The
Mass
Market
Woman

THE
Mass
Market
WOMAN

*Defining Yourself as a Person
in a World That Defines You
By Your Appearance*

◆

Linda McBryde, M.D.

CROWDED HOUR PRESS

This publication does not provide medical advice. It is sold with the understanding that the publisher is not engaged in rendering psychological, medical or other professional advice. If professional advice is required, the services of a competent professional should be sought.

Permissions
The author and publisher gratefully acknowledge the following artists and writers for their permission to reprint their work in this publication.

From "Woman" by Lillian Morrison in *If I Had My Life to Live Over, I Would Pick More Daisies*, edited by Sandra Haldeman Martz (Papier-Mache Press, 1992) Copyright © 1992. Reprinted by permission of Lillian Morrison.

From *One Writer's Beginnings* by Eudora Welty. Copyright © 1983, 1984 by Eudora Welty. Reprinted by permission of Harvard University Press.

Published by Crowded Hour Press. Eagle River, Alaska

Library of Congress Cataloging in Publication Data
McBryde, Linda M.
The Mass Market Woman:Defining yourself as a person in a world that defines you by your appearance.
ISBN 1-893070-06-9
LCCN 98-96650

ACKNOWLEDGMENTS

I would like to thank the many people who helped to make this book possible. To my husband, Brett, for his encouragement and faith. My children, Rory, Nolan, Connor, and Kelly, for their patience during "Mom's writing times" and for their cooperation in staying away from my computer files.

My editor, Sharon Goldinger, of PeopleSpeak, was invaluable as an editor and consultant, and she also proved to be a much appreciated source of encouragement and helpful information.

I would like to thank my friends who helped in many ways. To my dear friend Susan Travis, for commenting on the manuscript and for her enthusiasm and sincerity. Your faith sustained me in many a low moment. Thanks to my friend Cheri Spink, who inspired one of the stories in the book. I thank Susanne Patterson for reading the very early manuscript and Maria Shreve, M.D., for her friendship and encouragement.

My vision of womanhood could not have developed were it not for the circle of strong and beautiful women I am privileged to call family. So I thank my mother, Maureen Fedeson, M.D., my sister Laurie and sister-in-law Lora for the hours of conversation that have always helped me clarify my understanding of life, motherhood, and womanhood. My aunts, Rose Jordan, who has always shown me how love makes a person beautiful and Margaret Carol Kamon who encouraged me from afar. And to my sister-in-law Jodi, who is raising four spirited daughters—I thought of all of you often in the writing of the book.

TABLE OF CONTENTS

Preface xiii

SECTION ONE
UNDERSTAND THE BEAUTY CULTURE 1

1 Who is the Mass Market Woman? 5

2 Women are not products 8

3 Changing your looks will not change your life 10

4 It's not you, it's the beauty culture 12

5 Reject images of fashionable self-abuse 14

6 Fat phobia hurts us all .17

7 Have an opinion 20

8 Disregard beautiful fitness 23

9 Women don't age in the beauty culture 26

10 Does this really make sense? 28

11 Remember to ask why .30

12 Get the beauty culture out of your bedroom 33

13 If you threaten the beauty culture,
    it will threaten you back 36

14 Be wary of advice that reinforces beauty anxieties . .38

15 You have no need to compete with other women . .40

16 The beauty culture deserves to be laughed at 42

17 Sex is not a beauty sport 44

18 Change yourself; change the world 46

SECTION TWO

REMEMBER YOUR VALUES .49

19 Live as you will wish to have lived
    when you are dying 54

20 Trust yourself 56

21 You are real only to the people who love you 58

22 You have more important things to do 60

23 Appearance obsession
    prevents the more interesting you from showing . . .62

24 What counts more—
    being beautiful on the inside or the outside? 64

25 You don't deserve to feel bad about yourself 66

26 Just because everyone else
    is doing it doesn't make it right 67

27 Teach our daughters how to be women 68

28 Teach our sons about real women 70

29 Save your money 72

30 Has appearance improvement
    replaced life improvement? 74

31 Narcissism is boring 75

32 Beauty worship trivializes
    meaningful accomplishments 76

33 Consider the price of being attractive to men 78

34 Achieving peace with your body
    was not meant to take a lifetime 80

SECTION THREE

STOP SELF-CRITICISM

. 81

35 When you are at war
with yourself you can never win 85

36 *Satori:* suddenly enough is enough 87

37 Are you longing for validation? 89

38 Looking better doesn't necessarily
change your opinion of yourself 91

39 Be realistic—you're not getting another body 93

40 Self-criticism is bad for your health 94

41 Don't perpetuate
the cycle of judging other women 95

42 The world will see you as you see yourself 97

43 Men don't worry about this 99

44 Are you using self-criticism as female bonding? . . .101

45 Don't "mess" with your mind 103

46 Focusing on your flaws is selfish 105

47 Use thought stopping to end negative thinking . . .107

48 Attitude is everything 110

49 Peeves are not problems 112

50 Don't worry so much about how men see you . . .114

51 Time to grow up and out of body image concerns 116

52 Focusing on appearance
is a great way to avoid problems 118

SECTION FOUR
SEEK SELF-ACCEPTANCE 121

53 There is a reason why you are who you are 125

54 Reclaim the self-love you had as a child 127

55 Learn to appreciate "normal" again 129

56 Experience your body from the inside out 131

57 Be compassionate toward yourself 133

58 Stand in your own romantic spotlight 135

59 Be thankful for what you have 137

60 Act as if you are fine the way you are 139

61 Think about people
    you love for their inner beauty 141

62 Give your body credit for past performance 143

63 Want what you have .145

64 Recognize when you need professional help 146

65 Accept the admiration of someone who loves you .148

66 Don't spend time around
    others with appearance obsession 151

67 Find really beautiful role models 153

68 Find real women to be with 156

69 Appreciate yourself
    and you will appreciate others 159

70 Talk about it 160

SECTION FIVE

ENJOY HEALTHY SELF-IMPROVEMENT 163

71 Self-acceptance leads to healthier self-improvement 167

72 Keep your self-respect .169

73 "Not legal for trade" 171

74 Consider the cost of plastic surgery 173

75 Think hard about what
     really makes you feel beautiful 176

76 Express yourself through your appearance 178

77 Use your body to enjoy life 180

78 Let real life make your beauty decisions 183

79 Take care of your body .185

80 Use physical activity to feel better about yourself . .186

81 Eat something 188

82 Release conscious control;
     allow subconscious self-care 190

83 Respect your animal instincts 192

84 Get comfortable with your cycles 194

85 Respect the different stages of your life 196

86 Exercise your mind 198

87 Self-improvement
     should not cause emotional distress 200

Conclusion 203

Suggested Reading 206

PREFACE

The hotel swimming pool was alive with splashing children and lazy sun-worshippers as my sister-in-law and I
sat chatting. We had much to talk about because we live so
far apart, but our conversation soon turned to complaints
and little worries about our appearance. We commiserated
about finding time to exercise, noticing a few varicose veins,
and wondering if our husbands still found us attractive.

I watched the other women around the pool and noticed
how nearly every woman seemed somehow concerned with
her appearance. Two women and their husbands sat nearby,
the women discreetly covering their bodies with towels and
blouses. A pair of young women in bikinis glided past, glanc-
ing occasionally to see if anyone was watching them. Several
other women, poring over fashion magazines, carefully
arranged their bodies and their swimsuits to get the best tans.
A woman of about seventy with deeply wrinkled skin and a
muscular body strode across the deck, dove into the water,
and swam laps. Occasionally a well-coiffed and made-up
woman tiptoed into the shallow water, careful not to get her

hair or face wet. At the other end of the pool a handful of young mothers in one-piece bathing suits romped with children or performed water aerobic exercises. Two fully clothed women sat quietly by the edge of the pool, watching their children play.

Later, as I reflected back on our conversation by the pool, I regretted that we had allowed appearance worries to steal our precious time together—many more meaningful and enjoyable topics were left undiscussed. I was perplexed and sad that so many women of different ages, faces, and body types share this uncomfortable problem.

I have rarely, if ever, known a woman who was completely satisfied with her body or her appearance. Many seem to be always struggling to stay in control of their bodies. A few have achieved a tenuous compromise with their looks but dread the changes of age. For many women weight and appearance are excruciatingly painful subjects, as these issues have been for me in the past. For many years I suffered from an eating disorder and very low self-esteem, but over the years I have worked to change how I feel about my appearance, to feel more satisfied and less anxious, and to place health, beauty, and body concerns in proper perspective in my life. This book was inspired by, and the result of, those experiences.

The Mass Market Woman is about thinking differently and feeling more satisfied with our looks and our lives as women. It asks why women feel so much pressure and unhappiness about their looks, sometimes at the expense of feeling happy and fulfilled in other areas of their lives. This book serves as an inspirational guide to changing those harmful and unproductive feelings.

Throughout the book the underlying message is that you are more important than your looks, regardless of how much good looks are prized and rewarded in our society. This idea was the inspiration for the subtitle, *Defining Yourself as a Person in a World That Defines You by Your Appearance*. You deserve to feel confident that your accomplishments and personal growth are more important than losing weight or looking fashionable and that you do not matter less as a person because of your perceived weight problems or appearance flaws. It is not a denial of our feminine enjoyment of beauty and attractiveness but a reminder that these cannot be our first priority, especially when they cause us to suffer or compromise more important aspects of our lives.

The book—arranged in a series of individual essays—is divided into five sections, each dealing with a different area in which you can change how you think and feel about yourself. The essays are intended to serve as reminders, words of encouragement, and suggestions about the many ways you can think positive, healthy thoughts about your body and your appearance. You may want to reflect on how each principle applies to your own life.

The first segment of the book urges you to examine the beauty culture. If we understand the effects of media images of women and our society's very obvious preoccupation with youth and slenderness, we can begin to protect and strengthen our self-esteem by recognizing where our ideas about women's appearance came from.

In the second section we ask, Why has appearance improvement or weight loss become such a troublesome focus in our lives? What do we really value most in our lives? And most importantly, we can affirm our real values, such as love and virtue, developing our minds and talents and taking pride in our accomplishments, and let those values replace appearance anxieties in our lives.

Sections three and four, about stopping self-criticism and seeking self-acceptance, will teach us new ways of thinking about ourselves and remind us of the many reasons and ways to move from destructive thinking to positive, nurturing self-acceptance.

The fifth section of the book focuses on healthy self-improvement. The goal is to provide encouragement for us to care for ourselves—emotionally as well as physically—so that we are enriched, not burdened, by our goals of enjoying health, fitness, and beauty in our lives.

The Mass Market Woman will give you the tools to change your way of thinking about the media and the beauty culture mentality. You will find many of the essays are starting points for discussing the issues with your family, friends, daughters. The book is intended to give you the confidence and encouragement to feel better about yourself—not only about your appearance but about yourself as a person. I hope you will find the essays often support what you already know is right. And I hope they will help you to think about yourself and about other women in ways that are positive, empowering, and loving.

SECTION ONE

UNDERSTAND
THE BEAUTY CULTURE

UNDERSTAND THE BEAUTY CULTURE

The feeling that we need to look better or lose weight can easily take on exaggerated importance in our lives. The social importance of beauty for women strongly affects how we feel about ourselves. If we want to be deliberate about how we live or change how we feel, we first have to understand where our attitudes and beliefs came from. Where did we learn our ideas about what makes a woman attractive, interesting, or sexy? And why do we women so often feel desperately or triumphantly defined by whether we are thin, sexy, or fashionable? Why is this such a prominent part of our lives? Part of the reason is that we live in a very beauty-weighted culture, or simply, a "beauty culture."

The beauty culture could be described as the widespread social preoccupation with beauty and thinness for women that we see and hear every day. The idea that looking good is the ultimate achievement for women has been strongly commercialized by the beauty, weight-loss, and entertainment industries. We are so surrounded by subtle messages about the importance of a slender body or a pretty face that we hardly question them. Unfortunately, the effects of the beauty culture are also added to by the generations of women and men who have absorbed its values. Well-meaning family members and friends unknowingly perpetuate a preoccupation with appearance by commenting on our appearance or congratulating us on losing weight or sometimes even pressuring us to change ourselves "for our own good." They and we know there are more important aspects to our lives, but appearance often receives the most attention.

Certainly our ideas about women's appearances came from many sources—family, community, friends, our own experiences. But the prominent ideas about thinness, a sexualized look, and youthfulness seem to share a powerful common origin in the mass media.

This section on understanding the beauty culture will introduce you to some ideas about how the mass media—magazines, movies, television commercial advertising—influences our thinking. One of the concepts in this section, the concept of the mass market woman, is based on a problem most women are familiar with—far too often we compare ourselves to magazine models or television beauties used in marketing ads and feel we just don't measure up.

We can and should examine these ideas so we can begin to alleviate the appearance-based frustration that has become such a common experience for women. The concepts presented here will help us to understand the beauty culture and the mass market woman and encourage us to think critically about cultural ideas about women and beauty.

1

WHO IS THE
MASS MARKET WOMAN?

Who or what is the mass market woman? And how is she related to the problem of women feeling inadequate about their looks?

The mass market woman is the stereotypical woman that we see in the media used to represent optimal, desirable female beauty. She is an amalgam or a collage of the images of pretty girls and sexy women, or sometimes just female body parts, we see so often every day. We see these depictions of women in magazines, on television, in movies, on billboards. We are surrounded by them.

The mass market woman is not any one specific woman or supermodel; she is represented by many different women or girls, but she depicts the type of woman who is fashionable, acceptable. That is why skinny little Twiggy was as much a mass market woman as is voluptuous Pamela Anderson Lee. Each was marketed as the ideal woman for her time. A girl with that body type becomes a simple visual shorthand for "beautiful woman." The problem for the rest of us is that she becomes an almost exclusive cultural definition of how women should want to look. We start to believe that the women we see in the mass media represent the only acceptable way to be beautiful or lovable.

This standardized pretty woman is most often presented so enticingly that we can hardly help but compare ourselves to her. In a cosmetics ad her face is polished and youthful, free from any signs of worry or age. In a weight loss ad her body implies the blissful attainability of physical perfection. The ads usually imply that she possesses something we might want—a wonderful man, power, admiration, money, a great sex life. Whether she is used to sell lingerie, beer, or radial tires, her presence reminds us how greatly our society esteems this "look." Subconsciously, we may start to believe that if only we had breasts or legs like hers then we would have the love, attention, and possessions we crave.

Why do I call her the mass market woman? The mass market needs products and logos that are instantly recognizable. If you see double golden arches, you know you will get burgers and fries. If you see a trademarked bright red aluminum can, you know what the soft drink will taste like.

So if advertisers want to use a beautiful girl to attract your attention, they will not aim to represent a realistic sample of beautiful, normal women. Instead they will show you a logo woman—the same body type and the same face type used in all ads. Soon enough you will respond to this one kind of pretty woman. If you are shown all the many versions of female loveliness—including black, Asian, Hispanic, large, or mature women—the advertisers won't have a logo.

The mass market woman is an instrument of another rule of marketing—tell the customers what they want. Tell them over and over again. Soon customers will prefer what advertisers have encouraged them to prefer. The mass market woman becomes not only an advertising logo, she becomes the preferred product. Women begin to accept and believe in the loveliness of this stereotypical logo woman at the expense of appreciating their own unique beauty.

The next time you pick up a magazine or see a television ad, consider the reasons why we are confronted by these unrealistic images of women in the media. You will understand that women's dissatisfaction with their appearance is not inevitable; it is instead the predictable result of the mass marketing of beauty ideals. When you recognize that our cultural ideals of beauty are born of nothing more substantial than a marketing campaign, you can choose to look for more meaningful definitions of beauty for yourself. And you can begin to appreciate your own health and appearance without painful comparisons to the mass market ideals.

2

WOMEN ARE NOT PRODUCTS

When the mass market woman is used to advertise products to improve women, she is considered to be "proof" that the products work. A slender model proves a diet aid works. A mane of glossy hair shows us a hair product works. In a beauty product ad, a beautiful, new-and-improved image of a woman starts to represent woman-as-product. We are supposed to see our potential new, improved selves in her. "My wrinkles are gone. Yours can be too!" she tells us. "Look at me now—I've lost the weight. I'm a new woman. You can be too!"

More insidiously, though, these advertising messages affect our thinking about ourselves—in a subtle way, women begin to interpret these messages as proof that we women are improvable and in need of change. We start to think of our faces and bodies as if they were replaceable objects instead of parts of ourselves. Think of how fundamentally perverse it is for a human being to say "I hate my body," yet women say this and mean it all the time.

Women are indirectly encouraged to see themselves as products. Mass market products are identical, cheap, and attractively packaged. Women are encouraged to believe that with enough product improvement, such as dieting, exercise, or even surgery, we could look alike. How unreasonable it is that our individual differences are not respected—instead we are persuaded to correct our "problem areas."

Likewise, just as products are packaged to entice the consumer to pick them up, women are urged to use cosmetics and fashions to "Get the Look that gets the touch" and to know what the consumer prefers: "Gentlemen Prefer Hanes."

Many of us spend our whole lives struggling or grieving over our failures to remake ourselves into some acceptable version of the mass market woman. We need to stop and realize we are trying to solve the wrong problem. These attitudes and frustrations toward ourselves and toward women in general disrespect and devalue us as persons. We are not products, we are people. Our value, our interest, our desirability lies not in our packaging but in our hearts and minds; not in superficial, fashionable similarities but in our unique human differences.

Our bodies are not made of interchangeable plastic parts to be remanufactured—either by exercise cults or by scalpels. Our bodies are not just cheap packaging to be changed at will when they go out of style—they are us.

We can choose to step away from these harmful attitudes toward ourselves. We can ignore a culture that insinuates that we are only poor imitations of the mass market woman and instead enjoy our bodies, our lives, and our sexuality as whole, satisfied, and unique persons.

3

CHANGING YOUR LOOKS
WILL NOT CHANGE YOUR LIFE

The American writer Eudora Welty once wrote, "I had to grow up and learn to listen for the unspoken as well as the spoken—and to know a truth, I also had to recognize a lie." The beauty culture abounds with lies, spoken and unspoken. From the juvenile voyeurism of a beer commercial to the sincere girl-talk advice of a hair color ad, we are offered false promises:

> *The more beautiful you make yourself the better your life will be.*

> *If you can just lose weight you will be a completely new woman.*

> *You will be more exciting and fulfilled and you will have more romance, more friends, and more fun, if you can just become more beautiful.*

Learn to recognize the lies deeply embedded in our beauty-worshipping society. Only then can you recognize the truths that will allow you to improve your life. The beauty culture would have you believe fulfillment, love, admiration, and a worthwhile life all come to the beautiful people. To claim these prizes you must, as the Avon ad says, "Claim Your Beauty." Or you are promised if you lose weight on this diet plan, your whole life will change. The insulting implication is that you have nothing of substance or importance in your life that would not change with a mere twenty-pound weight loss.

All of these promises are lies. Stop wasting your time trying to be beautiful enough so that the world will come to you. It won't happen.

If you want to feel fulfilled, first determine where the unfilled areas are in your heart and in your life. Then get to work to create the life you want. Find work you love. Become the person you hope to be.

If you want wonderful, interesting people involved in your life, go find some wonderful, interesting people and get to know them.

If you want a more exciting life, start living. Take stock of your skills, analyze the goals nearest your heart, develop a plan, and start taking small steps toward a goal. None of these changes happen on their own—whether you are physically beautiful or not. The false promises of the beauty culture will not change your life. Only you can.

4

IT'S NOT YOU,
IT'S THE BEAUTY CULTURE

After the thousandth insult
she wakes up to fury

These are the opening lines of the poem entitled "Woman" by Lillian Morrison. How powerfully they capture the feelings of a woman who is ready to reject the beauty culture, ready to scoff at its thousand daily innuendoes about her inadequacy. She begins to ask, "How can I believe I must shackle my self-worth to my appearance when I see that my appearance changes daily yet my soul does not change?"

She shakes her head at the deeper insults of the beauty culture. The beauty culture says, "Be pretty. Be decorative in your sexuality or be unloved, unimportant." The message is a barbed hook swallowed by little girls who would rather be a Spice Girl than the woman who cures cancer. The message creates a fear that strikes deep. A mother will not nurse her infant for fear of changing the appearance of her breasts. Cosmetics outsell books. Eight-year-old girls are afraid to eat.

We look around us to see that men still have most of the power, most of the money. For men, money is power; power is power. Yet our women's magazines tell us, "Sexy is powerful." A hair spray ad assures us, "When you've got great hair, you know you've got the power to do anything."

Newspapers report the sexual harassment of women in the workplace while fashion magazines proclaim, "Working women's fashions are sexier than ever this year!"

How many times a day do you feel the pressure of our beauty culture? The demand that you become supermodel beautiful is scrawled out in bold headlines on magazine covers. "Trim your thighs," they insist. "Firm your butt. Perk up your breasts. Make your hair shiny. Correct your skin. Slim your waist. Disguise your age."

Before you spend another moment worrying about your looks, before you spend another day struggling with your body, before you critique another wrinkle, allow yourself a moment of skepticism. Admit that our culture is not sane about women, appearance, and sexuality. If you feel pressured about your appearance it is because you are surrounded by insanity. You are not at fault. You are not alone. Nothing is wrong with you. A lot is wrong with the beauty culture.

5

REJECT IMAGES OF
FASHIONABLE SELF-ABUSE

You may remember the movie *Splash* about a mermaid who falls in love with a man in modern-day New York City. In one scene Daryl Hannah, as the beautiful mermaid-turned-human, walks through a department store while a salesclerk shows her dresses. The chatty salesclerk gushes over Hannah's slim figure and adds that of course her daughter is slim too—"She's so lucky. She's anorexic." I cringed when I heard this, thinking of the painful realities for families of girls with anorexia. This was a light-hearted but thoughtless example of a common phenomenon—the media's endorsement of fashionably harmful ideals for women.

Many modern women are infuriated by a media culture that applauds anorexia, smoking, or dangerous diet pills as a means of achieving unhealthy physical ideals. Women today are aware that the fashion and beauty idols whom we are encouraged to imitate often purposely endure extremely unhealthy lifestyles to maintain their fashionable looks. Conversely, often the fashion idols are among the very small percentage of women who naturally have the revered body type—a body type most of us could never achieve even with the most desperate diet or even plastic surgery.

Some advertisers brazenly encourage us to sacrifice health for beauty. One cigarette ad, showing the body of a long-legged young girl, proclaims its skinny cigarettes are

"The slimmest way to smoke." The same company in another ad taunts us to prove we are feminine enough to smoke its brand: "Until you've tried walking in three-inch heels, you can't smoke one of ours."

We can and should object to this kind of advertising. Most women would rather enjoy their lives as healthy human beings than suffer to achieve unhealthy ideals. The sickness-as-beauty style of advertising deserves censure as was shown recently when certain advertisers promoted the heroin-chic image. Magazine and television ads featured gaunt, hollow-eyed models who looked like drug addicts selling products from jeans to perfume. Women quickly voiced their objections, and many ads were discontinued.

Some women show their disapproval of unhealthy media ideals for women by refusing to buy from certain catalogs or product lines because they object to the models used, many of whom are medically considered 10 to 25 percent under their ideal body weights. Others are very outspoken about how dangerous these social attitudes are—especially in a society in which an estimated one in four college-age women has an eating disorder. I am not trying to outline any one form of political activism on the issue—changing the way you think is your own most powerful form of activism.

Determine for yourself what seems unhealthy to you and how your own attitudes have been shaped. Recognize what damages your sense of self-worth. For example, we see so few women of average weight on television that seriously under-weight or anorexic women start to look normal and average weight begins to seem overweight. Recognize what types of marketing messages encourage or tempt you to risk your health, like the cigarette ads mentioned. Your health is more important than being model-slim. Please don't risk lung cancer or osteoporosis or chemical dependencies to slim down.

Work hard to clarify your perceptions. Turn off the television. Don't buy a magazine or product when you think the message is harmful. Concentrate instead on ideals that seem realistic and healthy to you and that allow you to redefine your own sense of beauty.

6

FAT PHOBIA HURTS US ALL

I recently saw a commercial on television for a laundry stain remover. The ad shows two women in a laundromat. One woman is older, probably post-menopausal, and quite overweight. She is wearing outdated pointy-rimmed glasses, a dated hairdo, and unfashionable clothes. The other woman of course is young, slim, and pretty. She has a short blonde casual haircut and is wearing a T-shirt that shows her shapely breasts.

The women spray their laundry stains with the two competing brands—the fat woman of course is so stupid she uses the "wrong" brand; the slim woman is smarter and uses the right brand. The attractive woman gets her stain out quickly and leaves. The fat, stupid woman is left sitting forlorn in the laundromat, rewashing her still-stained laundry.

After seeing the ad I thought, Gee, maybe the advertisers missed a few stereotypes about women. They forgot to imply that the obese woman was impolite, was gluttonous, and probably had vaginal odor. They forgot to imply the slim woman had a sparkling wit, great taste in interior decor, and saintlike self-discipline.

This ad was an obvious example of how unashamedly the media condones fat prejudice and how it uses fat phobia and stereotypes to dictate women's behavior. It was selling a laundry detergent! It was not even a product that directly benefits from fueling women's appearance insecurities, such

17

as a diet aid or skin cream. Yet the advertisers knew they could count on appearance prejudices that are so firmly entrenched in our social thinking that fat and slim and ugly and pretty comparisons are as clear as evil and good, dumb and smart, bad product and good product.

When we tolerate media messages like these that insinuate that fat equals stupid, graceless, and undeserving, we capitulate to social attitudes that pretend to know what we are like as people from how we look on the outside. If fat can be used to label a woman, then we are all vulnerable to labeling. Your pretty face may mean you are brainless. Your gray hair is taken as a sign that you are over the hill and incompetent. Your large breasts label you as an easy sexual conquest. All of these labels are unfair, and this thinking is not unlike the thinking that simply being female labels a person as inferior.

Remember also that a high percentage of body fat is a biologically female physical attribute. As a result of social dislike of fatness, normal female fat distribution and age-related changes have become considered abnormal and distasteful. If you find it hard to believe that these prejudices affect anyone except very obese people, let me give you an example:

I was once scheduled to administer anesthesia for a young, healthy woman for a simple operation. The preoperative information had been recorded by one of my colleagues. As I looked at the slim young woman on the stretcher, I checked to make sure I had the right patient—the record in my hand indicated "obesity." I asked my colleague why this five-foot-five, 130-pound woman should be medically labeled, in his opinion, obese.

"Well," he fumbled, "I did notice she had a little bit of a belly." The standards of unrealistic thinness cloud even the supposedly rigorous thinking of medical professionals.

Fat prejudice hurts all women. It makes life miserable for large girls and women. It sustains and validates other forms of appearance discrimination against women. It seeps into our cultural thinking, unchecked by concerns for fairness or legality, unhindered by the new "girl-power" kind of sexy pseudofeminism, unfiltered even by medical or scientific facts. Be aware of fat phobia in the media and mass culture. It hurts us all.

7

HAVE AN OPINION

While leaving a children's matinee one day, my children and I stopped in the theater's video arcade so they could play a game. Nearby, two little girls stood at one of the flashing screens. The girls were nine or ten years old—one with hair still in braids, both with lanky prepubescent bodies that were bony and sweetly awkward. The girls were playing a fairly tame video game of driving a race car through a crash course. At the end of the game the screen flashed to the "scores and winners" frame. On the screen were three men being awarded trophies by three ridiculously voluptuous, wild-haired women with watermelon-sized breasts surging out of their provocative string bikinis.

I couldn't resist asking the girls what they thought about these women. The girls shrugged uncomprehendingly and ran off giggling. Maybe the question was too embarrassing, especially from a stranger. Still, I worry about those little girls and all the girls like them. Most likely they didn't think anything at all about the wild bikini-clad women in their video game. Examples of these images are so prevalent, what is one more erotic image of subservient women on a game for children? Those girls will spend the next decade growing up exposed to a variety of images of women in cartoons, on television, and in movies. In these images they will see a confusing model of how women should look, act, and talk and what makes women popular or desirable. The worry is they may not think anything about those images either. Maybe no one will tell them they need to decide for themselves what makes a woman valuable. Maybe they will grow into women whose world-view and self-image are shaped by television, magazines, soft-core pornography, and cheap pop culture attitudes toward women.

As an adult woman interested in defining yourself as a whole person in that world, you should have an opinion about public depictions of women. The simple act of forming and holding an opinion is an act of power. It is your internal defense against the onslaught of images and attitudes that surround you.

You don't need to argue with anyone about this issue. You don't need to become the "morality police" for other people. Simply exercise and reinforce your own mental filter about the images you are continually receiving about the worth and meaning of a woman (and hence about your own worth and meaning). You will no longer be a passive recipient of pop culture opinions of women. You will become instead an active interpreter of your world. You might not want to try to change the world, but you can certainly decide for yourself what is reasonable and what is not.

For example, when watching films I have a much better opinion of a director who uses tact and artistic judgment in filming the female body. The director of a film that assails me with gratuitous titillation shots loses my respect. I no longer focus on whether my own breasts compare with those of the half-naked heroine in the movie. Instead, I wonder why the director has chosen to show such poor taste.

You are surrounded daily by a thousand subtle and not-so-subtle representations of what it is to be a woman in today's world. Exercise your power to decide for yourself what is an acceptable depiction and definition of a woman. In a world of media overload and morality-free electronic stimulation, you must be able to defend your mind against the influences that deflate your self-esteem and distort your ideas about yourself and other real-world women.

8

DISREGARD BEAUTIFUL FITNESS

The beauty culture confuses so many health issues. Thinness is confused with fitness. Well-applied cosmetic artifice is passed off as health. Anorexic models pose in sports equipment they are too weak to use. Women diet their breasts away then "correct" the "condition" with implant surgery. "Sexy" is defined in body fat percentages too low for fertility or libido. We read health and fitness tips from models who admit they never work out.

A culture obsessed with artificial thinness, giddy with the power to dictate the "appropriate" female form, has misappropriated women's desire to be simply healthy. The otherwise worthy goal of fitness is turned into yet another elusive beauty goal. In the cult of fitness chic, it is not enough to be fit and strong; a woman must also look slinky in a leotard. In fact, in the world of Beautiful Fitness, if all she does is look slinky in the leotard she is assumed to be fit and healthy!

It is great that sports and fitness are more accessible and available to women today, but unfortunately the beauty culture has introduced frustrating paradoxical ideals: a woman must be thin, taut, and muscular but not "too" muscular. She must strive for low body fat (often far too low for a healthy woman) but still have large breasts. A woman who is extremely fit but still has female fat distribution is diagnosed with "unhealthy" extra weight. The top female athletes will receive mass media attention for their perfomances only if they happen to look pretty as well.

The twisted message of the "fitness will make you beautiful" craze is that being fit, healthy, and strong will help a woman become beautiful, but she can prove her fitness only by becoming beautiful. The result is exercise fashions, exercise makeup, locker-room beauty anxiety. The garbled message is not "fitness is beautiful," which would make every woman potentially beautiful, but instead "beautiful fitness is beautiful," leaving us baffled again.

Is it any wonder you may feel depressed and resentful about pursuing your health goals or confused about whether fitness is worth the effort if you don't become "regulation beautiful"? Fitness is not the problem. Beautiful Fitness is the problem. Fitness feels powerful, wonderful. Beautiful Fitness feels frustrating and contributes to eating disorders and compulsive overexercising.

If you want to stop dreading the task of achieving unrealistic beautiful fitness, just start working toward real fitness. Focus on the basics: strength, endurance, and flexibility. Read about fitness conditioning from a reputable source. Join a well-coached women's sports club. Set realistic goals related to performance or enjoyment rather than weight loss or appearance.

Don't expose yourself to the gurus and disciples of Beautiful Fitness. Join a gym where people wear sweats, not thongs. Or don't join a gym, but sweat outdoors instead. Sign up for a women's run and look at all the different fit female body types. Watch fit old ladies whiz past you in spite of their natural female fat distribution. (The first time I stumbled through a half-marathon, I watched a woman of about fifty—short with very rounded, womanly hips—steam past me on a steep uphill stretch. I was inspired!)

Try this experiment: Watch the women in a triathlon on a sports channel, then quickly switch to a fashion channel; watch the models for a minute, then turn back to the triathletes. See any similarities? Of course not.

Fitness is fitness. Fitness is beautiful. Beautiful Fitness is a manipulative fantasy of the beauty culture. You can tell the difference, and you can make the choice.

9

WOMEN DON'T AGE
IN THE BEAUTY CULTURE

In the beauty culture, fear of aging is actively cultivated in the minds of women with the threat "You will no longer be beautiful (meaning loved, respected, worthwhile) if you show your age." The ideal woman of the beauty culture is not only ultraslender and air-brushed to perfection, but she is also very young. The only sanctioned image of a woman in the beauty culture is one who does not show her age. In fact, women in most fashion photography are not the ages they portray. Older women are played by wrinkle-free younger women. Grown women are portrayed by adolescent girls. The fashion industry dresses up children to show grown women what they should aspire to.

In cosmetics advertising, fear really sells, so the rejection of age is blatant. In a skin cream ad a young woman smiles slyly: "I don't intend to grow old gracefully. I'm going to fight it every step of the way." A model advises using a sunless tanning product: "Age this skin and I can say bye-bye modeling career."

Youth worship is also an insult to the grace and radiance of many beautiful older women. But more importantly, youth worship trivializes the important accomplishments of older women. As an intelligent, accomplished woman ages, her looks are often analyzed more than her abilities. Age should be about what you have done with your life, not about how well you have fought wrinkles.

The beauty culture defines maturity and age in women as undesirable; it assumes women should dread getting older and, by implication, uglier. Why should we accept this self-defeating ideal of youth as the only beauty? We are all growing older. Why drive ourselves crazy about something we cannot change?

Of course I am not suggesting we give ourselves over to early dilapidation. We will feel better, accomplish more, and remain independent longer if we stay strong and active and take care of our health. If we like to think young and act young, we can. Why not dress as young as we feel? We can use skin cream and youthful makeup if we want to. It really doesn't matter. The important idea is that we continue to like ourselves and care most about staying alive inside.

A sane, reasonable person deserves to be happy with her youth while young and happy with her maturity when old. These are simple goals grounded in reality. Yet these simple goals are a fulfillment missed by many women because of the endless frustrations caused by anti-age thinking. Don't allow your life to be frustrated and demeaned by youth worship. Don't allow hours of your life work to be supplanted by anti-aging beauty labors. Value your abilities and accomplishments. Be confident that the person you are inside can grow more beautiful with every year.

Be gentle with yourself as you age. When you look in the mirror, don't search for evidence that age has made you ugly. See instead the ways your age has made you complex, deep, and ever more alive.

10

DOES THIS REALLY MAKE SENSE?

Consider these common notions about men and women:

As they age, men get more handsome and women just get ugly.

Women just have to work harder to lose weight and look good than men do.

The most desirable body shape for women doesn't have hips, thighs, or subcutaneous fat.

Are these unfair but natural differences between men and women? Consider these "problems" logically. How can any of these possibly make sense in the intended scheme of the world? How could it possibly be reasonable that one gender of our species ages completely differently from the other? What mischief of nature could have caused one gender (males) to be adequate naturally but the other gender (females) to be genetically deficient, shaped "wrong," ugly, and in need of improvement? In what other species on earth is one gender not naturally attracted to the natural shape and appearance of the other gender? Unfortunately such non sequiturs are part of our cultural beliefs about men and women. Most people never stop to question them.

Now consider some historical ideas about men and women. In the Victorian era, few people questioned the widespread cultural beliefs about the moral, spiritual, and intellectual inferiority of women. People believed that higher education could make women sterile and that women simply didn't have the brain capacity for science. It was considered unfortunate but true that women needed men for moral guidance and to maintain their sexual chastity. These were accepted as the unfair but natural differences between men and women in that era.

Today we find these assumptions laughable. No self-respecting modern woman would live or limit her life based on these beliefs. Nor would she torment herself over her supposed intellectual, moral, or spiritual inadequacies.

What changed? Our way of thinking changed. A new way of thinking started with a handful of bold women who decided those assumptions about women were untrue. They knew those beliefs did not match reality.

Our way of thinking about beauty, desirability, and the natural state of our female bodies deserves a change, too. Why do we continue to torment ourselves over our supposed physical inadequacies? We deserve to see the natural, healthy female form as beautiful. We have the power to change our way of thinking about our bodies, our looks, and our lives. Someday women will look back and wonder why twentieth-century women worried about their looks and their bodies so much.

11

REMEMBER TO ASK WHY

Like many parents of young children I try to teach my children some critical thinking skills. I ask them questions about their reasoning. "Is that logical? Does it make sense? How do you know for sure?"

For example, my seven- and nine-year-olds sometimes stumble through an attempt at cost analysis. They ask me how much I paid for an item and then reflexively say, "That's a good deal!" I am flattered they think I'm a clever shopper, but I stop them, asking, "How do you know it is a good deal? What is the average cost of an item like this? Is it worth it?" What worries me is the likelihood they already suffer from consumer gullibility. They probably already believe that "If it is being sold, it must be good."

Like them, women must be careful about what they buy. The beauty culture depends on women being gullible consumers not only of lotions or potions or diets but also of ideas. The beauty culture sells ideas about what women really want, what men really want, what makes life enjoyable, meaningful, and worthwhile. It would not exist if women did not buy its ideas.

Reclaiming your mind and your soul from the beauty culture depends on your deciding which ideas are worth believing. You must decide the essentials in the life you want instead of automatically molding your life to the flimsy ideals of commercialized beauty.

If ideas are the products being marketed, women can become more critical consumers. For example, one idea is "You should be thin. You want to be thin. If you work at it you can be thin."

Begin the critique of this idea by asking, What is the product here? What is the price? Do I really need this?

Imagine a woman who, although a natural size fourteen, has her heart set on being a size ten. When she rigidly restricts her eating and works out religiously she can do it. She talks incessantly about her diet and will not eat with friends or family. She doesn't look that much different, but she fits into a size ten. She buys expensive fake foods. She thinks she looks sexier as a ten, but she is tired and hungry much of the time and has little energy for sex. Her husband likes her fine at her natural weight.

Ask her why she makes all this effort and she will tell you, "I like to be thin because then I look thinner." Does being thin have any other tangible benefits? Better sex? More energy? More love? More time for yourself or your family? If not, why did she buy this product—this idea about weight—again?

Another idea being sold is "You should be young. You should do everything in your power to stay young or at least look young." What is the price of this idea? The price is ever increasing dissatisfaction with ourselves. What is the product? The idea that you are not merely getting older, you are getting less desirable.

Is this idea sound or is it beauty culture trash? Older women are more financially secure. A woman's sex drive peaks in her forties or later, not before puberty as the blue jean ads would suggest. Women grow more secure in their self-images and in their networks of social support as they mature. As the rigorous but joyful years of childbearing pass, a mother may find more time for herself. If we see the positive changes like these in our own lives, why should we discount our own reality and prefer the artificial youth reality of the beauty culture?

We can judge for ourselves what is good and enjoyable in our lives. If we like ourselves the way we are, if we want to gracefully and gratefully accept our feminine bodies, then that is our choice. Let us thoughtfully decide for ourselves what we want.

12

GET THE
BEAUTY CULTURE
OUT OF YOUR BEDROOM

Do you love romantic movies? Recently I watched *A Walk in the Clouds*. It is a formula romance in a picturesque setting about fate drawing a man and a woman together. They must overcome the obstacles to their love. The characters are attractive and virtuous, and it is a pleasure to watch them fall in love. As the romantic and sexual tension between Paul and Victoria is building, they are in her family's vineyard one night trying to help the farmhands save the grape harvest from frost. They walk through the flickering light and smoke of the torches, their bodies nearly touching. You can practically feel Paul's breath in Victoria's hair, feel her shoulders against his chest as she walks in front of him in her nightgown. It is a great romantic scene—bodies close, hearts beating—full of tenderness and longing.

Where does the camera go next? Victoria's breasts. The scene is reduced from two yearning, blushing, palpitating people to two perky breasts. This happens three times in three long closeups.

Do you imagine the director considered using a long closeup of the man's crotch or buttocks for romantic emphasis? He would have considered it preposterous, I am sure.

I found myself wondering what the message was in this scene. "These are the breasts that made it all possible"? Or

"Here's a little entertainment for the men in the audience"? Or "However hot the sexual tension is, don't forget to worry about what your own breasts look like"?

The scene seemed to me such a perfect metaphor for society's obsession with women's bodies and what that obsession does to sex and romance. Women today have been raised on camera angles that follow the curves of the female body everywhere. We are so used to seeing only a perfect woman's body as the focus of any sex scene, it is no wonder we worry more about how we look than how we feel in our own romantic scenes.

This cinematic model of attraction between men and women based only on how a woman's body looks is not erotic, it's anti-erotic. It ruins potentially great sex and romance for many women.

One size does not fit all when it comes to romance. Men feel free to ignore the culture's beauty standards depending on what they love about the woman they adore. We women, unfortunately, are much more affected by its images because they can make us feel anxious that we don't measure up sexually. We can change that.

You don't have to believe your sexual attractiveness is determined by how closely you fit the beauty mold. A loving partner and a strong desire to please and be pleased go much further than perky breasts. Enthusiasm is much more exciting than perfection. Most men don't really want a woman as thin or as glamorous as we are told they do. Besides, not all men are perfect specimens either. Also, cultural standards of what is considered beautiful have varied widely from generation to generation and country to country. Real men have been loving real women since the beginning of time, but the stereotyped images of female sexiness we have been raised on are a fairly recent development.

Don't let those stereotypes ruin your love life. Get the beauty culture out of your bedroom. Focus on what belongs there—two people with bodies close, full of longing and tenderness. And don't change the camera angle.

13

IF YOU THREATEN
THE BEAUTY CULTURE,
IT WILL THREATEN YOU BACK

It takes courage to challenge the beauty culture. Most people have never stopped to question the idea that women
are supposed to care first and foremost about their appearance. Most people assume women are always trying to lose
weight or wishing they looked better, and that they have a
long list of improvements they should make to their bodies.
Try politely mentioning to someone that you don't diet, you
like yourself just fine, and you have more important things to
think about than beauty. Many people will treat you as if you
were crazy, or they might remind you that your beauty could
use a little work.

You may also experience the beauty culture's built-in
response for nonbelievers: your own attractiveness and sexual
desirability will be put on trial and your logic will be
described as sour grapes. If you object to the use of anorexic
girls in advertising, your criticisms may be interpreted as jeal-
ousy: "You just wish you were that thin." If you object to
gratuitous displays of female nudity in television and film,
you may be labeled prudish or reactionary. If you question a
culture that seems to prefer surgically altered female bodies
and two-dimensional pornographic sex over real women and
human intimacy, people may assume you are bitter and sexually frustrated.

It is not easy to change our way of thinking. It is even harder when our values are challenged by the simple-minded conformity most people live by. Don't give up. Keep working to define your own values for yourself; you can be instrumental in changing other people's attitudes as well as your own.

14

BE WARY OF ADVICE THAT REINFORCES BEAUTY ANXIETIES

The beauty culture perpetuates itself through advertising, through continual suggestions that you need improvement and for a few dollars more you can buy this improvement. No company spends millions of dollars to convince you that you are fine the way you are because if you feel good about yourself, you won't spend money to look better.

The beauty culture must continue to sell itself, even if that means intentionally making women feel insecure. This agenda is so pervasive in advertising and in women's magazines you might not even notice it anymore. The message that no woman is ever good enough is inserted into every nook and cranny of mass culture. We are told if we are feeling pretty good about ourselves, we are either kidding ourselves, lying to ourselves, or pathetically deluding ourselves.

I remember reading a self-help article years ago about common beauty myths. It cautioned, "Remember, if your husband or boyfriend tells you he likes you the way you are, he's lying."

It took me a long time to recognize this kind of advice for what it was—not friendly guidance from concerned editors of women's magazines but advertising manipulation disguised as helpful information. Advertisers don't want you to look for support from elsewhere because then you won't be desperate enough to buy more products.

When a woman is aware of these tactics, they seem like a laughable ruse. But when subjected over and over to the hints, insinuations, and insistence that we are utterly undesirable as women, our belief in ourselves is slowly chipped away. Eventually we accept it as a matter of fact, as unbiased reality, that we should look better—different, that is—if we can.

I once heard someone say, "If a strange man is walking out the back door with your television set at night, he is probably not the repairman." In other words, be suspicious.

When you read, see, or hear advice that makes you feel worse, not better, or hopeful but not satisfied, you should be suspicious, too. Acknowledge that the mass culture does not have your best interests in mind. Be wary of advertising, self-help articles, and other media messages that blatantly and insistently spread the message "Really, you're not okay."

Learn to recognize a thief.

15

YOU HAVE NO NEED TO COMPETE WITH OTHER WOMEN

The beauty competition mentality in our society makes women feel that we are constantly being judged for our looks. Many of us feel somewhat insecure (at least subtly, unconsciously) about our identities as attractive, sexually desirable women.

When we are constantly reminded by the beauty culture of our inadequacies, envy can become an unconscious reflex emotion. Sadly, we can even feel envious of our sisters or friends because this continual threatened feeling causes us to see all other women as potential rivals. We are even slyly reminded of this rivalry by beauty culture advertisers. "Don't hate me because I'm beautiful," says a woman in a makeup ad, implying that another beautiful woman is a threat to our relationships or social standing or that another beautiful woman makes us look plain in comparison.

What nonsense! We don't have to think this way. Freeing ourselves from beauty insecurities gives us opportunity and incentive to love other women as sisters and friends.

We can begin to throw off our fears and insecurities about body and beauty. We can refuse to participate in the frantic "jostling for random male attention," as Naomi Wolf so aptly phrases it. In so doing, we can refuse to see other women as enemies. As Wolf encourages in *The Beauty Myth*: "We can melt this suspicion and distance. Why should we not be gallant and chivalrous and flirtatious with one another? Let us charm one another with some of that sparkling attention too often held in reserve only for men: compliment one another, show our admiration."

If one deliberately chooses not to compete with other women about beauty, a vast resource of female camaraderie, attention, and bonding opens to us. Our deepest feminine urges tell us to sustain one another. We need the support, laughter, and wisdom of other women. Strengthening these bonds and enjoying our relationships with other women help to eliminate the unpleasant and harmful beauty competition mentality. We can instead appreciate beauty in ourselves and other women reasonably and joyfully.

16

THE BEAUTY CULTURE
DESERVES TO BE LAUGHED AT

Sometimes the beauty propaganda served up in the entertainment media is enough to make you laugh. The heroines often look and act more like lingerie models than role models. Ridiculous scenes seem to be concocted purposely to give the women characters a reason to shed their clothes or be glimpsed in the shower. Subtle and often contrived messages that seductive looks or deep cleavage is a woman's main source of power seem always present. But we, the women viewers, are expected not to question the silly scenarios or the messages.

We are supposed to believe that a woman would wear high heels and a slit skirt to go machete whacking through the South American jungles to find romance and precious stones. We are expected to believe there is a good reason why Indiana Jones's hard-drinking, gun-toting girlfriend would be silly enough to go cavorting through tombs filled with snakes and corpses while braless in a flimsy satin gown and high heels.

In the science fiction genre, we learn of an amazing intergalactic coincidence: alien females, even if they happen to have tentacles or heads like fish, also happen to have great breasts and long legs and know how to walk in stiletto heels. Imagine that.

Occasionally, some forward thinker in the media will make fun of the beauty hype for us in a movie or ad. For example, in the movie *In and Out*, Matt Dillon plays a local boy turned movie star returning to his hometown. Befitting his movie-star image, he has a blasé, chain-smoking, ultrathin fashion model at his side. Getting ready to go out for the evening, she casually reminds Dillon, "I need time to shower and vomit."

As they get closer to his hometown, Dillon looks forward to seeing his former student teacher, played by Joan Cusak, on whom he had a crush. He breaks up with the model at a motel; his parting words are "For God's sake, eat something. You look like a swizzle stick."

He meets up with his former teacher, who is a newly dieted, exercised, thin, and very hungry version of her former self. "But you were so beautiful the way you were!" protests the movie star to the teacher.

This light-hearted mocking of the beauty culture highlights the fact that an awareness of our society's appearance obsession is becoming more and more prevalent. More people are aware of beauty culture thinking and recognize that the director was making fun of it.

Laughing is one way to defuse and filter out the far-fetched sex-appeal worship found in the entertainment media. Keeping a sense of humor allows us to recognize the beauty propaganda yet not take it too seriously. If the mass media is the unofficial "authority" on the beauty culture, then, in the words of Hannah Arendt, "The greatest enemy of authority, therefore, is contempt, and the surest way to undermine it is laughter."

17

SEX IS NOT A BEAUTY SPORT

We live in a culture that suffers from a simplistic, juvenile view of sexuality. The prevailing mass cultural view of sex is that physical contact between two beautiful bodies makes great sex. We are brainwashed to believe we must have very slim, toned, perfectly shaped bodies in order to have great sex. The entertainment industry in particular offers a seductive visual paradigm for sex:

The better the bodies, the more passionate the sex.

Losing weight will improve your sex life.

Sex is only for the young and firm.

Mass culture has reduced and distorted our concept of human sexuality. Sexual relations are potentially the consummate act of human intimacy, an expression of love, passion, and individuality. But in our mass culture, sex is presented as a cross between a sport and a beauty contest.

This Beauty-Sport view of sexuality is a recipe for frustration and dissatisfaction for both genders, but especially for women. Women are burdened with the idea they should look like the sexiest possible version of the mass market woman in order to be desirable. Because they feel intimidated that men are comparing them to the mass media sex goddesses, women are often so worried about how they look they can't possibly enjoy their sexual experiences. These men and women get together, have experiences that focus on bodies and maybe orgasms but ignore intimacy, individual needs, and the specialness of each other as people. It is little wonder that these people have hollow experiences. To make matters worse, many women and men go on to interpret their sexual experiences through the Beauty-Sport paradigm of sex and decide that if only they or their partners had better bodies, then sex would be better. Women blame their bodies for their lack of orgasm, fun, intimacy, and love. Instead of discarding the Beauty-Sport idea of sex, they decide they are ugly or need to go on another diet.

Once again, changing our bodies is not the answer. Changing our ideas is the answer. Changing the ways men and women relate to each other is the answer. And to do that we must explore our ideas about communication, intimacy, and individuality.

As Dr. David Schnarch insightfully discusses in his book, *Passionate Marriage*, human beings take a very long time to reach sexual maturity. The growth of intimacy, not the "buffing" of the body, is responsible for the deepening of sexual experiences and the heightening of sexual enjoyment. Ultimately, a satisfying sex life is based on who you are as a person, not what you look like.

It is in our best interests as women, as people, to re-examine our ideas about our sexuality, why we feel so much pressure to appear and perform according to such false values about sex. Discard the Beauty-Sport paradigm of sex. Decide to respect yourself as a whole person and enjoy healthy, intimate sexuality as a part of a whole, healthy self-concept.

18

CHANGE YOURSELF;
CHANGE THE WORLD

" I wanted to change the world, but I found out the only thing one can be absolutely sure of changing is oneself." Aldous Huxley reminds us in this passage of a truth that we may each learn for ourselves in time. Many people protest that they cannot spend their lives trying to right the wrongs of the world. What they may not realize is they don't need to try to change other people, they need only start with their own minds. Buddhists have a saying for this idea: "Scrub your own doorstep." In other words, if you want to change the world, start right where you are.

One way the world needs to change is in its attitudes toward women—the crass mass market manipulation of feminine beauty and of the collective feminine consciousness. This would be a better world if women were not raised to feel imperfect, replaceable, and objectified and if the $30 billion spent every year on beauty improvement were spent to feed children, care for the sick, or promote social justice. It would be a better world if men and women saw each other as equals to be loved and respected, not as opponents, possessions, or entertainments.

Our society's beauty mythology is very powerful, and it creeps into our thinking about ourselves, our lives, and other women. But we are more powerful than society's myths. We can take charge of our own beliefs, relationships, and vulnerabilities. When we do this, we begin to change our society.

Buddhism teaches also that every human being is inextricably linked to all others. We are joined together with the fine threads of consciousness and the effects of our actions. When you begin to change your own way of thinking about yourself, the importance of your physical appearance and the intrinsic value of yourself as a woman—a person— you begin to change the world.

SECTION TWO

REMEMBER YOUR VALUES

REMEMBER YOUR VALUES

How can it be that a woman in our culture who gets everything "right" in life except appearance and physical beauty is considered a failure? Why is it that if a woman is loving, cheerful, courageous, smart, funny, and interesting, none of it matters if she doesn't have the right skin, hair, legs, and breasts? How can it be right that so many perfectly nice women feel bad about themselves?

How can it be right for us to base our self-esteem on characteristics we have so little control over—body type, size, breasts, legs? Why should we not instead base our self-esteem on characteristics we can control—our actions, thoughts, and ideals—attributes that contribute to a meaningful definition of self?

These are some of the questions you are already asking yourself if you are reading this book. You may be asking these questions because you are trying to raise a child, especially a daughter, in this slightly crazy world. You may be asking these questions because you have realized you want more than a lifelong struggle to lose weight or stay young looking. Regardless of your feelings about your own appearance, you may be asking these questions because you are concerned about how women are treated and valued in our society.

The questions you are asking concern a cultural phenomenon that many, many women are beginning to criticize and reject. It is the phenomenon of a widespread obsession with women's bodies and their looks in a culture that values women's appearance over their character and teaches them this standard from the time they are little girls. While women all along have quietly valued their accomplishments, they have also felt obligated to pay attention to their beauty and felt afraid of rejection if they did not stay "attractive."

It is increasingly evident in our world that we desperately need the contributions of women's skills, energy, and talent. The productive, creative, and interpersonal energies of the women in our society is a natural resource we cannot afford to waste any longer. But these energies are being senselessly drained through a siphon of beauty exertions and emotional battles with body image.

This section encourages us to focus on what is meaningful in our lives as a way of supplanting unproductive appearance anxieties. It reminds us that we have more important goals and values in our lives that should not be neglected for the sake of thinner thighs or a better tan. Several essays in this section also serve to remind us that through our attitudes toward ourselves we set an example for others—our daughters and sons, men and other women—and shape their attitudes toward women.

If we want worries about appearance to become less of a problem in our lives, we need to give ourselves permission to value our accomplishments over our looks; to improve our lives, not just our fashions; to exercise our minds, not just our bodies. Let us be judged for our lives, not our looks.

19

LIVE AS YOU WILL WISH TO HAVE LIVED WHEN YOU ARE DYING

Decide what you want your life to stand for because you are running out of time. Do you want to spend your last day on earth thinking about how much you hate your thighs?

If you want a life of vanity and narcissism or self-criticism and body anxiety, it is your choice. But don't waste your whole life while you're waiting for the day you finally look the way you want.

The age-old advice goes "Live as you will wish to have lived when you are dying." Think about what your thoughts are likely to be on your deathbed. No matter how self-obsessed you are, no matter how important your appearance seems to you now, your dying thoughts will not be:

> *If I were only a little better looking.*

> *If I had only been taller or blond or thinner, my life would have had more meaning.*

> *I just regret that I never had that tummy-tuck surgery.*

What you have right now, today, is this day and this body. No one on earth knows how many more days you will have to enjoy this day and this body and to do something meaningful with both.

The way you look is just not that important in the overall context of your life. If you are very lucky, you will be a wrinkled old lady when you die and may have learned this perspective from age and experience. Why not learn it now?

Today might be your last chance to live the way you want to live. Don't waste it on appearance obsession.

20

TRUST YOURSELF

Make a choice to think for yourself about yourself. It is the most important, life-affirming step you can take toward your future happiness. But don't expect it to be easy. It is difficult to feel confident deciding the problem lies not within you but all around you. All your life you have been hearing how important it is to look better than you do and how it is your fault if you don't achieve this glamour and happiness. It feels almost shameful to look around you for the source of your pain. Like many women, you may be more accustomed to blaming yourself and feeling inadequate. Your internal censor is ready with doubts and accusations:

> *Maybe I'm just really good at making excuses and just too lazy to make myself better. Maybe I am just looking for reasons to let myself go.*

> *Is my new attitude simply resentment? If I were a little thinner, a little prettier, would I be more content and live happily, beautifully ever after?*

> *Maybe I'm just exaggerating. I'm getting upset over nothing.*

> *I really don't know what makes sense anymore. Where do I count? How do I matter?*

It takes a lot of faith in yourself to disregard the messages that have shaped the way you feel about yourself as a woman.

Have faith. You are not making excuses. You are taking your first steps into a more sensible world. You are learning a new way of thinking about the rules of this very antiwoman social game of appearance discrimination. You are not exaggerating; you are just used to hearing women's complaints minimized. You do count because you are a human being. You are not lazy. You are not giving up on yourself.

You may wonder: I am starting to believe I am fine the way I am. I know I want my life to be more than a long struggle with my looks and my body. But how could I possibly be right and the whole rest of the world be wrong? Take courage from my favorite line from Ralph Waldo Emerson: "Trust thyself. Every heart vibrates to that iron string. Nothing is at last sacred but the integrity of your own mind. Absolve you to yourself and you shall have the suffrage of the world."

Trust your instinct to find deeper meaning and values as a woman in this culture. Believe wholeheartedly in yourself and everything that you are.

21

YOU ARE REAL ONLY TO
THE PEOPLE WHO LOVE YOU

Basing your self-esteem on meeting the approval of the anonymous impersonal judgments of the beauty culture is a mistake. If you think that you would be happier with yourself if you could just meet with general public approval, you are wrong. The simple but harsh fact is the world does not care about you. And it won't care more about you if you become more beautiful. You may receive accolades for achieving socially sanctioned beauty, but they will have nothing to do with who you are as a person. It's not love, it's just attention. That kind of attention is not for you as a person; it is for you as an icon, a symbol of the beauty culture, an object. Whether you are beautiful or not so beautiful or in between, don't base your self-concept and personal meaning on the anonymous opinions of the general public.

Instead, you must build your self-concept around the kind of person you are and the love and support of the people who love you. See yourself through the eyes of people who have proved they love you no matter what you look like. Your family and friends care about you, and the kind of person you are to them is much more important than how you look to an impersonal world that doesn't know you. If you are beautiful to these people, nothing else matters. And beauty in the eyes of love is not subject to the "rules" of the beauty culture.

You may get a smile from this passage from *The Velveteen Rabbit* by Margery Williams about love and becoming Real. In the story, two nursery toys, the Rabbit and the Skin Horse, talk about what it means to become Real, which is what happens to toys when they are truly loved by someone.

> *"Does it hurt?" asked the Rabbit.*
>
> *"Sometimes," said the Skin Horse, for he was always truthful. "When you are Real, you don't mind being hurt."*
>
> *"Does it happen all at once, like being wound up," he asked, "or bit by bit?"*
>
> *"It doesn't happen all at once," said the Skin Horse. "You become. It takes a long time. That's why it doesn't often happen to people who break easily or have sharp edges, or who have to be carefully kept. Generally by the time you are Real, most of your hair has been loved off, and your eyes drop out and you get loose in the joints and very shabby. But these things don't matter at all, because once you are Real you can't be ugly, except to people who don't understand."*

Consider the sweet moral of this story as you confront the pressures that divert us from meaning in our lives. Resist the pressure to focus on your beauty at the expense of your relationships. The idea that glamour is more important than being loved is wrong. Remember the message of *The Velveteen Rabbit:* you are beautiful and real to the people who love you.

22

YOU HAVE MORE
IMPORTANT THINGS TO DO

Focusing on your appearance saps your energy. It steals your time. It prevents you from focusing on all the more enjoyable or more important things you could be doing. The more you worry about your looks, the more time you devote to calorie counting, wrinkle prevention, and split-end repair, the less time you have to exercise your talents productively.

When you focus on your looks as a daily life goal, you are cheating the world of your creative energies by paying too much attention to yourself. And this process is a vicious cycle. The less time you spend producing, creating, and doing, the less capable you are of producing, creating, and doing. If you spend all your time trying to achieve perfect abdominal muscles or a perfect tan, you are missing time to improve your poetry, your cello playing, or your volunteer work. Before you know it, you have nothing to offer but your abdomen and your tan. The world doesn't need more great abs and tans. It needs more poets, cellists, and volunteers.

This lesson is illustrated in the movie *Alice.* Alice is a rich, dissatisfied wife who spends her days in a pampered routine of manicures, coiffures, and massages. She knows there must be more to life and more to herself but still wonders if she can find it in a new skin lotion. Through her bizarre encounters with a Chinese mystic and his magical herbs, she learns she can shed her old life and her meaningless routines. The end of the movie shows Alice in jeans and an old sweater, happier than ever, having reconnected with her adoring children, working for the homeless, and having fulfilled a life-long dream of working with Mother Teresa. We hear the voices of her clueless former cronies: "Have you seen Alice Tate? She looks better than ever!"

Unlike Alice, you don't need mystical herbs to redirect your energies. You do need to believe you are more than your looks. You have something important to offer. Don't waste it.

23

APPEARANCE OBSESSION PREVENTS THE MORE INTERESTING YOU FROM SHOWING

Endlessly slaving away to refine your appearance fills your days and your mind with trivialities. The more time you spend working on your outside, the less time you have to develop your inside. Spend too much time posing and primping for the fickle eyes of the beauty culture and you will forget to engage the world with your mind. Mary Wollstonecraft expressed this idea so poetically over a century ago:

> *Taught from infancy that beauty is woman's scepter, the mind shapes itself to the body, and roaming round its gilt cage, only seeks to adorn its prison.*

This idea is illustrated in the movie *Little Women*. The youngest daughter, Amy, wore a clothespin on her nose, trying to reshape it. Finally, the usually gentle Marmee (her mother) scolds her vain and pretty daughter Amy for being "more interested in fashioning your dear little nose than developing your character."

When your thoughts are on pointless body obsessions, or narcissistic details, you become bland. The next time you realize you are thinking more than you should about appearance, think about what you can do to develop your personality, your intellect, your spirit. Exercise your virtues. Share your expertise. Improve your talents. Correct your character faults. Show more of what you are on the inside; worry less about the outside. Be more patient or funny or daring or creative. Be yourself. Stop wishing for the perfect body and show more of your interesting self. Take the clothespin off your nose for the day.

24

WHAT COUNTS MORE—BEING BEAUTIFUL ON THE INSIDE OR THE OUTSIDE?

"**B**eauty is only skin deep" our mothers and grand-mothers were cautioned. "Pretty is as pretty does" our great-grandmothers may have heard. These old sayings become clichés because of the truth in them.

Every woman would probably agree it is more important to be good and kind and loving than good-looking. Then why do so many very nice women feel depressed about themselves? The first reason is the positive reinforcements our society provides to those considered beautiful. People are nicer to them. Men look at them. Women friends compliment them. Second, we have internalized a lot of the social reinforcements for looks. In other words, when you know you look good, even if no one is complimenting you or looking at you, you imagine they must be admiring you.

There just aren't many external reinforcements for being a great person. We tend to treat good character as a consolation prize for not being pretty enough. But why don't we have more internalized reinforcements? Why doesn't it feel as good to be a nice person? It is because just being nice isn't enough to reward us; we have to act. We can't cling to the knowledge we are good people underneath—we have to touch people's lives.

Dale Carnegie taught people to always make one nice, genuinely kind or concerned remark to everyone you meet.

Don't walk out of a room without having given someone a compliment, said something meaningful, asked a concerned question. Don't stop at hello. Deepak Chopra teaches people to send their positive emotional energy out to people through a gift, a compliment, a prayer.

You don't even need to be extroverted. Norman Vincent Peale, if he couldn't say or do something nice for people, would "shoot prayers" at them, often complete strangers. He would say a simple little prayer asking God to ease their burdens or send a little happiness their way.

Try this and you will immediately start to feel better about yourself. This practice of being kind and thinking kind thoughts has many rewards. Some of the rewards are practical: you will make friends, kindness becomes its own form of charisma, people will remember and appreciate you, you will make other people happy.

Some people would say this practice just makes you feel good. Others understand it as the love of God being shared. Still others experience it as a karmic circulation of positive energy. Whatever you want to call it, kind actions build your psychological reserves, build your self-esteem, and make it feel worthwhile to focus on developing kindness and character.

These are the rewards to fill the void between looking good and "just being a nice person." In the long run it is much more fulfilling than imagining whether strangers are admiring your looks.

25

YOU DON'T DESERVE
TO FEEL BAD ABOUT YOURSELF

Why do so many women spend their lives feeling unhappy about themselves? If you are one of them, consider that the reasons you are unhappy with yourself—if they are beauty reasons—are probably not rational at all. You don't deserve to feel bad about yourself because of how you look.

How can it possibly make sense in a world filled with crime, abuse, and hatred for you to suffer serious doubts about your self-worth because of your appearance? Think of the truly malicious acts people are committing in the world. Hurting people, polluting the environment, committing child abuse, and stealing are crimes to feel guilty about. It makes no sense for you to feel guilty or unworthy because you like cream cheese on your bagels or because you can't seem to blow-dry your hair quite right. It is ridiculous and unfair for women to spend so much of their lives feeling tormented over things that are so irrelevant in the grand scale of humanity.

In this world it is hard enough simply to be a good person. In the eyes of God it has always been good enough to be a good person. Don't lose sight of this fact worrying about how you look to a frivolous and sometimes deeply troubled world.

26

JUST BECAUSE EVERYONE ELSE IS DOING IT DOESN'T MAKE IT RIGHT

In a sex- and status-driven culture, it can seem almost reasonable to think about our looks most of the time. "Dress for sexy success" is a business directive. Youth and sex are the standards for appearance blazing from every billboard, television, and computer game. Surrounded by women who are caught in the same frantic whirlwind of frivolous or desperate beauty and image concerns, we spend too much energy thinking about how to look better, dress better, or attract more men because almost everyone around us is doing the same. As a result, thinking about appearance becomes so automatic we aren't even aware of it. No one else notices it either because they too are busy worrying about their looks.

But doing things because everyone else does them is usually a mistake. Many people are unhappy, shallow, and unfulfilled because their lives revolve around appearance and status. This is not to say you can recognize unhappy or shallow people by their appearance—that attitude is exactly what we are trying to get away from. But if your relationship with your appearance is leaving you unhappy, shallow, and unfulfilled, it is your responsibility to rethink it. When you find a way of being in this body, in this culture, in this world that allows you to be yourself, you will most certainly stand out from the crowd.

27

TEACH OUR
DAUGHTERS HOW TO BE WOMEN

I have a friend, Julie, who is very petite, slender, and effort-lessly feminine in her appearance without paying any attention to clothes or makeup. As her first daughter was growing out of toddlerhood, it became apparent little Jennifer would be built more like her daddy—tall, muscular, athletic, and big.

Julie tells me how seriously she takes her responsibility to raise Jennifer with a good self-image. She does not want her to feel compared with her very petite and feminine mother. She is also acutely aware of the possible discrimination and negative messages Jennifer may get as she is growing up. She may have mixed feelings about her wonderful, strong body as she receives the social messages against strong, big, and tall women. She is heartbreakingly likely to feel ambivalent about her developing body.

Julie is a wise woman. She resolved early to monitor her own speech, actions, and attitudes. "I never criticize myself in front of her," she says. "When I exercise around her, I make sure we talk about health and getting strong, not about need-ing to look a certain way in a bathing suit." Julie knows she is the first and strongest model of female identity for her daughter. Jennifer will probably not look like her mother, but she will almost certainly learn to think like her. Julie's atti-tudes toward feminine appearance and the roles of women as real people, not just sex objects, are strong defenses Jennifer will carry with her in life.

Learning from her mother and other women who see themselves and all women as more than pretty decorations will reinforce this little girl's sense of self.

This affirmation of feminine acceptance should be passed on not only between mothers and daughters. Embracing and appreciating your feminine self is a gift you can give to all our daughters, the women of the next generation.

Virginia Beane Rutter expresses this idea beautifully in her book *Celebrating Girls*: "A single affirmative action between a woman and a girl on behalf of the feminine ripples out to larger and larger groups of girls and women in our culture."

When you show our daughters that you respect your body and take pleasure in your feminine self, "the ripple of female affirmation continues to spread."

28

TEACH OUR SONS
ABOUT REAL WOMEN

With three sons and all their little muddy friends and an open-door policy, I usually have a lot of little boys in my house. I have thought a great deal about raising boys in our modern world, so I was horrified to watch the following television commercial with my husband and sons, who all adore baseball.

> *A group of small boys is gathered in the dugout after a baseball game. Their coach is consoling them after a lost game and asks them where they would like to go to eat. The place with the clown? The other burger place? The boys are indifferent. Finally one boy whoops, "Let's go to Hooters!" The coach lights up with a lascivious smile as the other boys all cheer. "Hooters! Yeah!"*

This commercial is a disturbing example of the media messages our children are exposed to and of the world in which we parents are trying to raise a generation of decent young men.

These young men are yet another reason to dissociate yourself from beauty obsession: your sons and other boys and young men in your life need to see in you an example of what a woman can be. Young boys, the men of the next generation, need to learn about real women. They need confident, happy women, more alive than the flat characters with big busts on television. They need hugs and encouragement from real women who are warmer than the glossy, posed, two-dimensional figures in magazines. Boys must learn from accomplished women with heart, not the vicious vixens in video games. They need to understand about real women with rights and feelings who are making love and making babies and making lives with real men who have rights and feelings, too.

Reclaim your own sense of self from the plastic ideals of the beauty culture. Then share yourself with your sons and mine. Open your heart and mind to as many young men of the next generation as you can. Be a mother, friend, or mentor. Talk to boys about media images of women in cartoons and television. Monitor what they watch on television. Share your understanding of a woman's life and her body. Teach young men about love and fairness, sexuality, and the diversity of women as real human beings. Don't let them learn it at Hooters.

29

SAVE YOUR MONEY

Think of all the money you may have wasted over the years on impulse purchases of clothing and cosmetics. (I know I have been guilty of quite a few of these in the past.) These desperation purchases were often of items that didn't really suit your tastes. They may have been cosmetics or clothes that weren't really your favorites, but you bought them because in some small way you hoped they would change you or make you look a little more fashionable, slender, or pretty. Sometimes, just for a moment, you believe the advertisers' unrealistic claims. Even a sophisticated cynic once in a while purchases on an unrealistic beauty impulse. Later the useless article ends up under the bathroom sink or in the back of your closet.

I am not suggesting you shouldn't buy clothes that make you feel wonderful or use cosmetics and affordable luxuries you enjoy. Quality clothes and little luxuries are not a waste of money. What is a waste of money are the purchases you make because advertisers' tactics made you dislike yourself and hope the products you buy will improve you. Whether you believe the products will actually make you better or whether you plan to simply enjoy the products makes all the difference. You want to spend your money on something you will enjoy, not lose your money to a deception.

When you confidently choose to appreciate your natural qualities and admire a broader range of beauty, you become immune to the advertising–induced paranoia that makes you feel you need to spend large amounts of money to correct your flaws. You become less susceptible to those urges to buy products that promise to change your genetics, perfect your inadequacies, stop time, and fulfill your hopes and dreams. Save your money.

30

HAS APPEARANCE IMPROVEMENT REPLACED LIFE IMPROVEMENT?

Think of five or ten or twenty ways you would like to improve your appearance. Make the list as long as you like. From coloring your hair or firming your bottom to growing your nails longer. Take your time. Be honest. Have fun. Include a few whimsical desires. Focus on changes that will really improve your appearance.

Are you finished with the list? Now cross off each item one by one and in its place write a personal life goal—a way you would like to improve your mind, your personality, your skills, or talents. Take your time. Be honest. Have fun. Include a few whimsical desires. Focus on changes that will really improve your life.

If you were able to think of ten ways to improve your looks but unable to name as many life goals, you may have been allowing beauty concerns to supplant personal growth. You may have been allowing your interest in your appearance to supplant meaningful self-improvement.

Don't worry if you are not sure yet about your personal goals. The beauty culture has worked hard to define your beauty goals for you. The personal life goals you'll have to develop by yourself.

31

NARCISSISM IS BORING

It is unpleasant being around someone who can't stop talking about herself. You know the type. She is constantly analyzing her hair, her weight, and her cuticles. She wants to share with you her latest deep thoughts about hair highlights or nail strengthening. She has long stories about her latest weight loss fling. She not only wants to tell you her calorie count for the day but also wants to count yours. Fashion magazines and catalogs comprise the bulk of her literary experiences. She spends long hours in quiet contemplation of the various merits of pore cleansers. This self-absorption not only bores other people, it also takes up the mental space she could be using for more interesting and provocative thoughts.

If this character is you, you need to free up some mental energy for more important or enjoyable thoughts.

If this is someone you know, don't waste much time listening to such drivel. It might give you bad ideas.

32

BEAUTY WORSHIP TRIVIALIZES
MEANINGFUL ACCOMPLISHMENTS

By holding beauty as the ultimate triumph in life and sexiness as the trophy of beauty, the beauty culture trivializes the real, meaningful accomplishments in the lives of women. Take, for example, a recent magazine article, "Real Life ER Beauties." In a ridiculous piece that seems to be life trying to imitate television, emergency room doctors and nurses were interviewed about their beauty tips. Some of those men and women have over a decade of higher education and daily hold life and death in their hands, yet they were being complimented on their hair and nails.

In the same article a female neurosurgeon was interviewed about how she keeps her complexion so nice. I think we should pause and think about that for a moment: Do you know how many years of specialty training it takes to become a neurosurgeon? About ten. Isn't that more impressive than her skin care routine? Would you care about dry skin lines on someone who had an electrocautery knife in your cerebral cortex?

In another article in the same magazine, a news reporter quips laughingly that she owes her career to concealer. I think she deserves a little more credit than that.

When Uta Pippig raced to victory in the Boston Marathon, I distinctly remember the commentator remarking about how great Uta's hair still looked after 26.2 miles.

Someday when I accomplish my goal of completing a marathon, if anyone says anything about my hair, I might become violent.

This appearance-obsessed mentality in our culture is so pervasive we sometimes hardly notice how thoroughly and methodically it serves to devalue and minimize our real accomplishments in life. Important goals and achievements are shuffled to the background; beauty secrets become what are important.

One of your personal challenges may be to give your own accomplishments their due importance. Allow yourself the dignity of taking credit for your achievements, talents, and hard work without apologizing for your beauty flaws. And don't ever deceive yourself that beauty achievements alone can make a life.

If you put on a few pounds getting through graduate school, it should not minimize the satisfaction you feel about your accomplishment. If you are the mother of small children, you are doing the hardest, most important job in the world. You don't lose credit for not being glamorous. There are many areas in life in which to define yourself without letting beauty judgments get in the way. Don't let appearance obsession trivialize your life.

33

CONSIDER THE PRICE OF BEING ATTRACTIVE TO MEN

Thankfully, single women these days are not assumed to be woeful spinsters holding their breath until a man comes along to turn them into whole people. Nor is it assumed that the only reason for a married woman to keep her looks nice is to keep her husband from shopping around. Still, the question arises: How important is it to you to be attractive to men (or a man)? Is attractiveness, like nice clothes and good grooming, just a part of the whole picture of "you"? Then that's great. Or are you sacrificing a large part of your time, your thoughts, your individuality to make appearance a central focus in your relationships? Once again the important question is, How are you defining yourself?

Many women slave away mindlessly to stay looking as if they were twenty. Or they exert phenomenal grooming efforts to try to match the dominant mass media view of what is considered desirable by men. These women think physical attractiveness is the only way to attract a man, or they fear someone younger or prettier will steal their man. This idea becomes a self-fulfilling prophecy. If the only attribute you develop is good looks, then your looks are what men will judge you by among other women. Do not ever give up everything intriguing and unique about yourself in a doomed attempt to keep ahead of the competition because if a man wants a younger, prettier woman, he will find one somewhere.

It takes a great deal of effort and concentration to grow into your best potential self. Health of mind and body are linked; work toward both and you will be quite lovely. If a man you love feels it is worth his while to love a sane, unique woman in a healthy body, he has made the right choice, and so have you.

Remember the original story of the Little Mermaid by Hans Christian Anderson. The little mermaid sacrifices her voice to change who she is and become human to win her Prince Charming. The prince never falls in love with her as a human because he was in love with the girl who he thinks saved him from drowning. Because she has no voice, the mermaid cannot tell him the truth: that she herself rescued him while she was still a mermaid. She dies alone and lonely. She never gets her prince because she couldn't tell him about her real self.

34

ACHIEVING PEACE WITH YOUR BODY WAS NOT MEANT TO TAKE A LIFETIME

I am absolutely certain that in the great cosmic order of the universe, liking and enjoying your body was not meant to be such a huge problem. When you consider the immense spectrum of emotional, intellectual, and spiritual accomplishments of which humans are capable, being comfortable with your body seems like a rather elementary life skill.

Expecting a task to be difficult is often a self-fulfilling prophecy, so if you think it's nearly impossible for you to be satisfied with yourself, you will find it nearly impossible. Instead, treat self-acceptance as a simple and fundamental task so you can accomplish it and move on.

You are a spiritual being inhabiting your body for a given number of years on this earth, in this life. Accept the fact that this is the body in which you will accomplish the rest of your humanity. There are many sensual pleasures you can enjoy through your body; of course these include your appearance and your sexuality. But these are just parts of the gift of human experience. Body and beauty and sensuality are wonderful. But they are not everything.

You must acknowledge you are only a tiny speck in the cosmic order of the universe. You must admit that your physical appearance is a tiny transient part of your life, a partial expression of your spiritual self. You can then relegate the task of accepting your body to its proper priority in your life.

SECTION THREE

STOP SELF-CRITICISM

STOP SELF-CRITICISM

" Our greatest foes, and whom we must chiefly combat, are within." So said Miguel de Cervantes. The one most important step you need to take to empower yourself, to redefine your sense of yourself, is to stop criticizing yourself. Beauty culture thinking trains us to be our own worst enemies. When we hear how imperfect we are as women often enough, self-criticism becomes part of our own internal dialog. Continually confronted by manufactured images of what we are not, we feel there must be something wrong with what we are.

Our own judgments about our beauty often determine whether we feel lovable, desirable, and feminine, so it is easy to feel desperate about our weight, faces, breasts, or hair. Confronted daily by the untruth that if we only tried harder we could be thinner, prettier, better, we may mistakenly employ self-criticism as motivation. Self-criticism should never be mistaken for motivation—instead of building you up, it tears you down. There are plenty of reasons why you should not engage in unhealthy self-criticism. It is bad for your self-esteem and bad for your life. The stress of negative thinking is also harmful to your health.

In this section we will think about the reasons why we criticize our looks and our bodies. Is it a habit or a disguised plea for validation or even a form of female bonding? We will also consider the social implications of appearance obsessions: We do not want to implicitly criticize other women or perpetuate the cycle of judging women by their looks. Besides, men don't feel the need to worry so much about these issues; why should we?

Next, we will discuss your being realistic about the body you have and the fact that criticism changes nothing. In this section you will learn some strategies for stopping the habit of self-criticism. "Thought stopping" is an extremely effective method. Refocusing your attitude and being realistic about the unimportance of little flaws is also immensely helpful. Start now to stop self-criticism. Begin today to eliminate this self-destructive way of thinking from your life.

35

WHEN YOU ARE AT WAR
WITH YOURSELF, YOU CAN NEVER WIN

What do you do when someone despises you? How do you react to someone who criticizes and berates you or is always trying to change you? How do you feel about this person's rejection or stingy, provisional approval? Are you yielding, cooperative, and receptive to her? Are you inspired to perform your best? Do you feel empowered, strengthened, and supported? More likely, you feel minimized, discouraged, and depressed. Your reaction is likely to be resistance or betrayal or outright defiance.

Unfortunately this pattern of derision and opposition reflects the relationship many women have with themselves. We criticize our bodies, our genes, our will power. We chastise ourselves for our imperfections and weaknesses.

How can you find the courage and will to become your best physically, mentally, and spiritually if you don't believe you can? Who will encourage you in your darkest, most painful moments if not you? You can't even good-naturedly laugh at your own foibles and peculiarities if you are always on the defensive—and the offensive—with yourself!

To be and feel your best in your life and to make worthwhile improvements in yourself, you need first to value your true inner self, be gentle with yourself, respect your body, mind, and soul. But more than that, you need to give yourself positive messages.

These messages are called affirmations—literally telling yourself what you want to believe about yourself. Using affirmations is a method of getting the conscious and subconscious parts of your mind to agree. With affirmations you can remind yourself you're okay, you're a nice woman, and you're worth liking.

Find phrases you are comfortable with and that are meaningful to you and repeat them to yourself. These affirmations need not be forced or formal; you don't have to sit in a funny position to do them. Remember, an affirmation is not a thought to be pounded into your head nor is it a chant with which to hypnotize yourself. It is simply a deep slow breath of thought and a gentle reminder that you believe in yourself. Stop the negative messages. Try an affirmation like one of these:

> *I love myself.*
> *I know I am a good person.*
> *I accept who I am.*
> *I respect myself and the process of my life.*
> *I am peaceful and harmonious within myself.*

36

SATORI: SUDDENLY
ENOUGH IS ENOUGH

Satori is a Japanese word that refers to experiencing a new way of seeing or understanding. It is used by Zen masters to describe a moment of enlightenment or newly acquired awareness. Though in English we might refer to a paradigm shift, or maybe a breakthrough, these terms do not capture the intensity of the experience of *satori*.

In her wonderful book *Breaking Point*, Martha Beck, Ph.D., describes the *satori* experiences of women who come to a breaking point in their lives when they begin to see clearly how their lives—their true inner selves—have been compromised, suppressed, and distorted by perceived social rules and paradoxical role demands. Transformed by this often-painful shift in perspective, a woman who has been through *satori* is ready to write her own "rules."

Beck's book discusses women's experiences in redefining their self-concepts in many aspects of their lives—family, marriage, career, and social roles. In a similar way, a life-changing shift in perspective is something many women experience in coming to grips with their long struggles with body image and appearance obsessions. For some women this shift occurs as a sudden turning point or crisis in a life-long pattern of self-criticism, eating disorders, or beauty addiction. For other women it is a slower process of coming to realize the pointlessness of the never-ending struggle to adapt to an unobtainable cultural ideal of flawless beauty and perpetual youth. For others it may be an indefinable, haunting feeling that something must be wrong about feeling so much pressure about one's appearance.

My personal turning point in my understanding of my appearance obsession came in my twenties. Throughout my teenage years, I envied the rail-thin models in magazines and struggled with stringent diets and exercise to try to change my average, muscular build to fit the wispy, fashionable ideals I saw. After a decade of tortured self-image and years of bulimia, I found myself struggling with depression and bulimia more than ever during my first year of medical school. I realized that if I did not conquer at least the outward, functional disturbances of my eating disorder, I would fail a very important class. Hypnotherapy helped me to stop the bulimic binges and purges, but my poor self-image persisted. My *satori* about body image came later, years into my relationship with the man who is now my husband. During a particularly obsessive mood, I writhed in self-hatred and self-pity over my perceived body flaws. As he sat helplessly witnessing my senseless self-loathing, he quietly said, "You know, this is the only thing I really don't like about you." Something deep inside me realized I could lose my soul and my soul mate to the same problem. Something had to change. And it wasn't my body.

37

ARE YOU
LONGING FOR VALIDATION?

Is criticizing or belittling yourself the only method you know to ask for support or positive reinforcement from others? Are you consciously or unconsciously waiting or hoping for others to contradict you when you complain or criticize your body?

The beauty culture sanctions only certain versions of female body parts and body shapes and has convinced too many women not to trust their own judgment about female beauty and certainly not to trust themselves about the worth and loveliness of their own bodies. A woman who feels comfortable and healthy at an unfashionable weight is embarrassed to admit she feels good, so she dutifully criticizes her body, waiting for someone else to tell her she is okay.

A woman who secretly finds her average breasts sensuous and her unremarkable abdomen exquisitely erotic (even though they don't fit the beauty culture standard) doubts her own opinion. She can't believe her body can be and feel so wonderful since it doesn't match the glossy images she sees everywhere. The woman resorts to criticism of her "faulty" body parts, knowing she shouldn't have to, but deep inside longs for appreciation. She wishes someone would tell her what she already knows—"You're fine the way you are."

She feels healthy and beautiful and harmonious in this natural female body. Instinct tells her this body was intended.

But faced again and again with a culture that contradicts her beauty, she becomes anxious, resigned, defeated. Modest or ashamed of her pride, she compares herself to the meaningless beauty blueprints. She can only wait for someone else to give her back her beauty and her self-appreciation by contradicting her complaints and forgiving the "beauty flaws" she feels compelled to point out.

Stopping this type of self-criticism starts with a moment of daring to doubt the validity of the beauty ideal. There are so many kinds of beauty, so many subtle qualities in each of us. We deserve to love what we see in the mirror, without apologies or comparisons to the impersonal mass market ideals. There is quiet rebellion in deciding "I like myself. I trust the way I feel. I am beautiful the way I am."

38

LOOKING BETTER DOESN'T NECESSARILY CHANGE YOUR OPINION OF YOURSELF

It is an interesting irony about appearance and self-esteem that how women feel about themselves does not necessarily correlate with how they look. In other words, attractive women don't necessarily feel great about themselves and less attractive women don't necessarily have lower opinions of themselves. Improving your appearance won't automatically fix the way you feel about yourself.

More proof of this fact is the number of young, professionally beautiful women—actresses, dancers, models—who have eating disorders or are depressed about their weight or about aging. The most important influence on how they feel about themselves is not whether or not they are beautiful—they certainly are—it is how much pressure they feel over the need to be and remain beautiful. It is because in their professions they are defined by their looks. Appearance takes on an exaggerated importance in their lives.

Most of the women I know who feel good about themselves are mature and by most standards not as attractive as they were ten years earlier. Yet they are much, much more secure in themselves than they were in their tight, taut, stretch-mark-free days. These women have come to feel better about themselves with every year, clearly not because they look better but because they do not define themselves by their appearance. Being at ease with their physical selves comes not from having perfected their looks but from having the opportunity to do something with their lives and to work toward the goal of becoming a better person.

In your life you have a choice as to whether you will be defined by your looks. It is up to you to choose what your defining values are. Feeling good about yourself can then depend on how well you live up to those values, not on how well you maintain your looks.

Being responsible and loving and raising your children well is an accomplishment that time or gravity or a weakness for double-cheese pizza can't take away from you. Being generous and sensitive and a good friend doesn't come in a bottle. And you don't have to starve, squeeze, paint, or pluck yourself in order to live up to your highest values and become the person you want to be.

39

BE REALISTIC—YOU ARE NOT GETTING ANOTHER BODY

One woman I talked to gave me her nugget of clarity on the topic of women and appearance: "At some point, you just don't see the use of worrying anymore. I mean, you are not getting another body, right? You start to realize that who you are is just who you are."

This is an important but simple truth. Keep a realistic perspective about your appearance. Body type, bone structure, and other genetic factors are yours to keep; you might as well make the best of them. Give yourself permission to accept them. What else can you do? Some features you can change, some you can't. How much time and energy are you going to waste resenting what you cannot change? Struggling against reality, denying who you are and what you look like, leads only to resentment and frustration.

Work instead to find a cheerful, humorous, contented attitude toward your appearance. There is only one you. As the ancient poet Rumi said, "Make a way for yourself inside yourself."

40

SELF-CRITICISM
IS BAD FOR YOUR HEALTH

Focusing on what you don't like about yourself is not healthy. Negative emotions such as anger, anxiety, and resentment create stress that is very damaging to the body. Not only do medical studies link anger and resentment to heart disease and high blood pressure, but they have also begun to show that chronic emotional stress even shortens your life.

When you are frustrated, unhappy, or even angry with your body and your looks, your body produces hormones and chemicals as your nervous and endocrine systems respond to the stress and tension. These substances contribute to a host of physical ills and prevent you from maintaining a sense of well-being.

Breaking this habit is not only good for your physical health but also good for your emotional health. Stopping self-criticism is a prescription for both emotional and physical well-being.

41

DON'T PERPETUATE THE CYCLE OF JUDGING WOMEN

Do you remember back in the 1980s when the movie *10* came out? In the movie, Bo Derek played a woman who was considered so gorgeous that she was ranked ten on a scale from one to ten. While the movie was popular, one-through-ten scoring became a sort of pop culture shorthand for judging women's looks. Men would wink knowingly to each other and casually cast numerical judgment on passing girls and women. As a sensitive modern woman you would never dream of encouraging that kind of foolish thinking. Unfortunately, you might be unintentionally doing just that when you criticize your own looks.

When you criticize your body or talk excessively about disliking your appearance, you perpetuate the social habit of judging women by their appearance. When you complain about your figure flaws publicly, you are implying to others you think it is reasonable to criticize women's bodies for figure flaws. If you berate your own breasts, legs, or hips for not looking like the official, mass market, beautiful-body standards, you are also berating all women who don't meet the standards. By judging yourself, you encourage women to continue judging themselves and others by their looks.

Unknowingly, women do this all the time. Offhand comments such as "I can't believe I weigh this much!" or "What I wouldn't give to look like that!" are a message to other women. The message is, "I'm not okay and neither are you."

Appearance appraisals in the coffee or locker room just deepen the grip of the beauty culture. A coworker moans about her "fat, disgusting thighs." Every woman in the room cringes, wondering one more time that day whether her thighs also are too fat or being painfully reminded she, too, is "disgusting." One woman judges herself as lacking, and all other women in the room are coerced into the same attitude about themselves. Who feels self-confident enough to speak up against these judgments? Who dares unless she has an officially sanctioned beautiful face or body?

You will hear women try to stop this nonsense, saying, "Oh come on, you look fine." They are really trying to say, "Please stop criticizing yourself because if you don't look fine, then neither do I. And neither does anyone else here." Women do not want to be forced to agree that they should not feel good about themselves unless they fit the ideal.

Not only should you stop saying these critical remarks but you should stop thinking them. If you mentally compare yourself to the mass market woman, you are comparing all women to this ideal. You are carrying the belief inside you that some women are more valuable based on their appearance. Your belief in these comparisons will show itself in your attitudes toward all other women, the way you view media images of women, the way you raise your children, the many ways you live your life. Don't do this to yourself or to other women. The next time you refrain from public displays of self-criticism, you are doing it for the good of all other women as well as yourself.

42

THE WORLD WILL SEE
YOU AS YOU SEE YOURSELF

Consider this very important psychological dynamic: people will come to see you as you see yourself. If you think of yourself as a loser, someone unattractive or unaccomplished, you will behave that way and others will also begin to see you as such a person. But if you see yourself as someone powerful and beautiful, loving and loveable, this is the person you will show to the world. Your mental self-image influences how you present yourself, how other people think of you, and how they interact with you.

Thinking positively about yourself is a good habit to develop. Likewise, thinking negatively about yourself is a bad habit you simply must get rid of. Practicing positive thinking is very much like exercising a muscle—keep doing it and you will make it stronger and more sustained.

Focusing on a belief in yourself as an admirable and loveable person—one who is attractive and feminine just as she is—is a powerful way to help other people to see you that way. If you see your character qualities—your humor, kindness, intelligence—as your most important assets, others will adopt your focus.

In a like manner, if you believe there is more than one way for a woman to be beautiful and attractive, your own unique physical assets will begin to shine for others. There really is no rational reason to believe a woman has to be skinny, tall, and white with a 36C chest and chiseled facial features to be considered beautiful. If you believe petite, freckled, and muscular is beautiful, it is. If you love your wide-hipped, voluptuous, dark, curly-haired self, people will begin to notice how lovely you actually are.

Define yourself as a person by measuring yourself against more meaningful values than your appearance—kindness, generosity, humor, inner peace. Choose also to appreciate the qualities in your appearance you want others to appreciate. When you have learned to see your inner as well as your outer being in the most positive way, the world will also see that person.

43

MEN DON'T
WORRY ABOUT THIS

Can you even remotely imagine a book like this written for men? Can you see men writhing in the kind of appearance angst most women consciously or unconsciously live with? Imagine a burly construction worker sincerely admitting, "I just have to accept that this is how I am built," or a pinstripe-clad executive asking, "Do you think this makes me look fat?" Picture a college-age guy explaining, "When I start to get dizzy, I know I have to eat."

The unfair truth is men don't agonize at all about their looks. They get a haircut every other month and shave grudgingly every day, but that is about it. Women have full-length mirrors, vicious three-way department store mirrors, and a little hand mirror so they can wince at the back view, yet most men, as a male friend tells me, do the "shaving mirror test." A guy stands in front of a mirror that shows only his face, flexes muscles he most likely doesn't have, sucks in his potbelly, and confirms, "Yeah, I'm a stud." And he really believes it! He doesn't become morose watching the chiseled body-builder in the Soloflex ad—Stud is in the kitchen getting more beer and chips. And he would never compare himself to the handsome male models in the deodorant-soap commercials—he thinks if they were real men they would be sitting on the sofa watching television, not acting on television.

Not only do men have no trouble accepting themselves, but they usually think they are more attractive than they are. I remember hearing about a survey once that concluded the majority of men rate themselves as above average looking. Meanwhile perfectly lovely women are in psychologists' offices trying to learn to accept their hips and their hunger.

Again and again I have found that the question, "Would this seem fair if a man had to do it?" is a reliable litmus test for social inequities. It is a worthwhile question when dealing with appearance anxieties, too. Men can go through life not worrying about these issues. Why shouldn't we?

44

ARE YOU USING
SELF-CRITICISM AS FEMALE BONDING?

Women need other women to talk to, to give and receive advice, to share their feelings and stories. Psychologically, women draw strength from shared experiences, understanding each other and themselves. This sharing is wonderful and healthy. But there is one way in which this kind of female bonding becomes unhealthy—when it is communal self-criticism.

You can hear women doing this all the time in locker rooms, ladies rooms, and offices. They share conspiratorial confidences about stretch marks and wrinkles, calories and workouts. Wistful beauty commiseration has become the standard fare for girl talk.

Maybe beauty commiseration is not entirely bad. Sharing and talking about our worries with women friends can make us feel better about ourselves. And sometimes the girl-talk self-criticism is completely in jest as women joke about how ridiculous it is to worry about all these minor flaws. Those types of talks help us to remember we are all human and not in competition.

Conversations about appearance become a problem, though, when they make us feel worse. When we start to feel the only appropriate way to talk about our bodies or our looks is to apologize or criticize, it is not healthy and it is a poor excuse for female bonding. When we complain about our bodies' normal features, we reinforce unrealistic beauty criticisms of women. When we talk about cellulite or some other very normal female body feature, the message we give each other is too often, "Don't worry, I have the same problem." A much better message would be, "Don't worry, it's not a problem."

The next time you find yourself talking to women friends about appearance or health, be sensitive to whether the talk is supportive and realistic or whether criticism has become an unhealthy substitute for real female bonding.

45

DON'T "MESS"
WITH YOUR MIND

O ur personal histories of beauty miseries are sometimes
talked about in the strangest places. On a long week-
end on call, the residents' lounge in a pediatric hospital was
where Pam and I swapped stories. We probably started talking about how hard it was to find time to exercise during
residency. We tiptoed around the subject of losing the few
pounds we had gained on cafeteria food and long hours of
working. Each of us cautiously confessed our refusal to diet.

At some point in a conversation like this, a woman
knows if it is safe to get serious. Pam confided that although
she was heavier than she wanted to be, it was a lot better than
when she was anorexic. She filled in the details. Her story
was not unusual, but it ended with her at eighty-four pounds
in the hospital. She explained further her refusal to diet. "I
was pretty miserable back then. I would like to lose some
weight now, but I'm really careful not to get too uptight
about the weight issue. If I think about it, I can get really
obsessive. I'm just really glad I didn't die, and I don't want to
mess with my mind."

The point of my story is not to emphasize the destruc-
tiveness or prevalence of anorexia but to share with you
lessons some of us have learned the hard way: Don't dwell
on appearance issues that make you feel miserable. Don't
take your health for granted. If appearance is taking on an

exaggerated importance in your life, then don't focus on it. Don't overdose on the toxic amounts of glamour worship in magazines, on television, or in your environment. If trying to lose weight makes you instantly neurotic, don't try.

In your quest to feel like a whole person, regardless of your appearance, your mental serenity is what is most important. Whatever you do, don't "mess" with your mind.

46

FOCUSING ON
YOUR FLAWS IS SELFISH

No one wants to admit to being vain or narcissistic. Yet some women who would disdain spending all day admiring themselves will have no qualms about spending the same amount of time criticizing themselves.

You may rightly insist it is not selfish to focus on flaws you want to improve or change, and of course a little objective self-assessment now and then is necessary and good. Examining your physical self to find your strengths and your weaknesses and deciding what needs work is completely reasonable. But if you are spending considerable amounts of time and emotional energy staring at the mirror hating certain body parts or vowing you are never eating again, then you are wasting your time in a very self-centered and unproductive manner.

Constant self-criticism is self-centered because it prevents you from thinking of other people and their needs. It deprives the world of your other creative energies and meaningful thoughts. Imagine if Mother Teresa had spent time agonizing over her wrinkles or her body. Could you imaging orphans being turned away at the door with "I'm sorry, she can't help you today—she's having one of her self-loathing days"?

Remind yourself not to be selfish. Don't think about yourself—especially negatively—all day long.

This is not to say you do not deserve time to focus on yourself. Learn instead to be selfish in a positive way that replenishes your energy and emotional reserves. Meditation, sports, hobbies, and even a little luxurious pampering in reasonable doses are healthy ways to focus on yourself. Use positive actions to replace the destructive and selfish habit of self-criticism.

47

USE THOUGHT STOPPING
TO END NEGATIVE THINKING

I used to be the Queen of Negative Thinking. I could turn a bad hair day into a week of suffering. If I gained a few pounds I thought my world was about to end. A pimple could send my self-esteem crashing through the floor.

When I decided I didn't want to spend my whole life feeling bad, I intuitively realized I had better stop thinking bad thoughts. I was very lucky in one respect—I seem to have a loud-and-clear connection with my own inner voice. I could hear the derogatory thoughts starting and I could force myself to think about something else.

Interestingly, those negative thoughts, when you stop them, don't go underground and fester. Instead, they usually just go away.

As I began to learn how valuable my "thought stopping" was, I read a bit more about the subject. This is some of what I learned:

"Cognitive restructuring" is the technical term for this process, which helps people to change or retrain their thoughts to have a positive effect on their behavior and feelings. Inside our heads, we all talk to ourselves. Some people hear this inner voice clearly and easily and are aware of what their thoughts are "saying" to them. Others are barely aware of the sometimes terribly hurtful things they are saying to themselves deep within their own minds.

You can make yourself feel miserable about your looks, reinforce your obsessive concerns about your appearance, or feed your anxieties about losing your looks by allowing your mind to continue dwelling on its harmful self-talk such as this:

I never look as good as other women.

I'm so fat.

If I'm not beautiful, I'm nothing.

I'm getting old and ugly.

It doesn't matter if these thoughts seem objective—if the words and tone are hurtful, you need to stop them. Damaging your self-respect in the name of truth accomplishes nothing; it does not even motivate you to change your behavior.

The first step in stopping your destructive inner thoughts is learning to really listen to your inner voice. Try to hear what you are saying to yourself about your appearance. The next step is to identify the derogatory words or phrases, such as "I have to be," "I'll never be," "hate," or "ugly."

Once you are aware that a thought needs to be stopped, silently tell yourself Stop! until the thought is squelched. The earlier in the thought you stop it, the better. This will be easier once you recognize your most persistent thoughts. These recurring thoughts are the most damaging. Stop them at all costs whenever they occur.

Once stopped, the negative thought must be replaced by a more positive one. Give yourself something helpful and nurturing to think about, but don't make it a weak generalization. For example, if you hear yourself think, I always feel so ugly at parties, you can't just substitute, I feel beautiful at parties. Instead make the replacement thought realistic and constructive: "I am dressed really attractively tonight. People seem to enjoy my company at parties." Pretend you are talking to a friend. What would you say to encourage her?

This technique of thought stopping and switching is a tool you can use forever to help you take charge of your thinking. Learn to use it if self-criticism has been preventing you from having the positive attitude and self-respect you deserve.

48

ATTITUDE IS EVERYTHING

It is not likely that while you and I are alive the world will suddenly stop judging women by their looks. No matter how well you care for your health, how clear and meaningful your priorities are, or how virtuous you are, there will still be appearance discrimination toward you as a woman. Fat women will still be demeaned and rejected. Pretty women will still get attention for everything except their brains. Cleavage will definitely still sell beer.

Appearance discrimination is part of our social and corporate culture. We know this. Women will still lose jobs based on their looks or age or weight. Prejudice and misogyny will not die easily.

We can try to educate others, defend ourselves legally, conduct ourselves with aplomb, and change what we can. But there will still be plenty of opportunities to feel upset or disappointed because of appearance discrimination. Then what?

Then what you must rely on is your own attitude.

Viktor Frankl, in his book *Man's Search for Meaning,* teaches the most profound lesson on attitude you will ever read. Tortured, starved, and brutalized in a Nazi concentration camp, he sustained himself with this ideal: "Everything can be taken from a man but one thing: the last of the human freedoms—to choose one's attitude in any given set of circumstances, to choose one's own way." When we reflect on the overarching human significance of Dr. Frankl's message, problems with self-acceptance and resentment of society's appearance obsessions seem minimized. His experiences and personal strength certainly make self-esteem problems seem manageable, even petty.

I realize, though, for many, many women the problems of social pressure and rejection based on appearance are neither minimal nor petty. Their lives become constricted and painful. I believe Dr. Frankl's teachings can be of tremendous help. Read *Man's Search for Meaning*. Exercise your freedom to choose your own attitude.

Choosing your own attitude is more than just a way to face the beauty culture with your head held high. In the end nothing will tame the beauty culture as effectively as a world full of women with positive attitudes about themselves.

49

PEEVES ARE NOT PROBLEMS

In a culture that is fixated on appearances, we worry far too much about how we look. This burdensome awareness of appearance can make your imperfections seem more important than they really are. Your perceived flaws seem magnified. Little improvements you haven't accomplished or haven't made time for feel like glaring faults. Whatever our individual appearance imperfections are, under the constant pressure of beauty awareness, we sometimes treat them as if they were problems, not minor peeves.

It is important, though, to remember the distinction between problems and peeves. Problems include sick children, friends in trouble, and marital difficulties. Peeves include dry skin, "figure flaws," and wrinkles. It is not right that women feel so much pressure about their looks that they worry about their peeves as if they were problems. And it is not right to unbalance our lives with worries about "problems" such as female thighs that leave us emotionally drained for our real lives.

I am not by any means suggesting that the average woman assigns more importance to a broken nail than she does to a sick friend or that women are vain or confused enough to worry about their hair instead of doing their taxes. On the contrary, it is amazing that most of us women accomplish what we do—keeping the whole juggling act of work, families, and all our other responsibilities in order—

and still manage to find any time to stay in shape, fix our hair, and look nice. One woman even suggested to me that if men had to handle all that women do and then still shave their legs, pluck their eyebrows, and struggle with blow-dryers, beauty standards would be lowered in a big hurry!

What I am suggesting, though, is that the large number of times per day that women feel compelled to wonder about their appearance is a burden. I suggest that the weight and appearance problems we have been convinced we have are blown so far out of proportion that we need to work intensively to change our thinking about them. I suggest we can drastically reduce the number of problems in our lives by redefining our appearance issues as peeves and saving our energy for more important problems.

50

DON'T WORRY SO MUCH
ABOUT HOW MEN SEE YOU

If you are concerned about your looks because you want to be attractive to men (or a particular man) you probably shouldn't be so hard on yourself. In the first place, men do not see women the way women see women. Men do not analyze women as negatively as we tend to.

In an informal consultation with several experts (meaning I asked my husband and several male friends), I learned male attraction is more general than you might think. In other words, the male brain is more likely to think, Hey, she's kinda nice, or a more Neanderthal response might be, Ahh, a female.

So quit worrying about the details so much. Men aren't perfect either. You don't find all men attractive. Not all men will find you attractive either, but some will.

"But," you may object, "men do want physical perfection from women! They want *Baywatch!*"

It is true that many men have developed a fetishistic attraction to centerfold-perfect visions of women. These men, after years of exposure to intensive mass marketing of the female body, develop a syndrome all their own, which Dr. Gary Brooks analyzes in a disturbing but enlightening book, *The Centerfold Syndrome.* Voyeurism, objectification of women's bodies, the need for sexual validation, and fears of intimacy comprise most of the serious personal disturbances in this kind of man. These men are not the best candidates with whom to start a relationship.

While no man is totally immune to this force-fed obsession, most men have reasonable expectations of women and are capable of intimacy with nice, ordinary women. Men who see women as objects for decoration and for sexual entertainment are not worth women's time and interest.

You don't want a relationship with a man who does not see you as a whole person. If you need to convince yourself of this further, just look around you at people and their relationships. Some people, men and women alike, readily admit that appearance is immensely important to them in a relationship. They are usually shopping for a third spouse or ending another short-lived relationship. Remember, as Goethe warned, "No confusion of the real with the ideal ever goes unpunished." A man who is looking for the ideal mass market woman is looking for a well-packaged product, not a person. Stay grounded in the knowledge that the only man worth your time is one who is interested in you as a whole person.

51

TIME TO GROW UP
AND OUT OF BODY-IMAGE CONCERNS

If you have had body-image frustrations for years and years, maybe it is time to grow out of them. It is distressingly common for women's feelings of physical inadequacy to have started during adolescence, when we first realized we were becoming women and all the mass media obsession with female bodies was now about us. But we don't necessarily have to cling to those body-image frustrations. Your emotional defenses were not mature during adolescence, so you were more susceptible to feeling inadequate. As a mature woman you have years of experience and accomplishment to buffer your negative feelings and adolescent body obsession. You can decide it is time to give up those feelings.

I read somewhere that if you are the same person at forty that you were at twenty, you have just wasted twenty years. As the years pass, if you are not changing, you are not really living; you are just stagnating. Likewise, if you have the same body complaints year after year, you are wasting a lot of emotional energy and achieving nothing. You can make the choice to regard your dissatisfaction with your appearance as an outdated, immature mode of thinking. Body woes are useless; you might as well discard them.

Or look at the problem another way: If you have had the same complaints about your body for the past five, ten, even twenty years, then either do something constructive about them in a self-loving way or forget about them. Complaining about and disliking yourself for these features or problems hasn't changed them. It must be time to change tactics. Besides, you have obviously become who you are and done what you have with your life in spite of those "flaws," so maybe they aren't really such big problems after all.

Perhaps women in our culture will never completely escape coming into womanhood with some feelings of imperfection and inadequacy. However, we can decide that body-image concerns are not a necessary or unavoidable part of a grown woman's life.

52

FOCUSING ON APPEARANCE
IS A GREAT WAY TO AVOID PROBLEMS

Quite a few years ago I heard some female acquaintances discussing a woman friend who was completely neurotic and obsessed with her weight. They felt sympathetic toward her because it appeared her husband was always pressuring her about her weight, always suggesting she lose twenty pounds so she would be more sexually attractive to him.

One woman bitterly proclaimed, "I would gain twenty pounds and never sleep with him again."

Another frowned and said, "I would lose the twenty pounds and still never sleep with him. Or better yet, I'd lose the twenty and sleep with his best friend."

It is a true story, and if it made you laugh, I can understand why. But I hope you recognize the bitterness, the irony, and the mixed messages these women were giving each other and themselves.

The problem in this woman's life, deep down, almost certainly had nothing to do with her body. However, the point of my story is not to analyze this couple's marriage but to point out how frequently our bodies get blamed for our problems. Clearly this couple, who focused on the woman's weight as a barrier to intimacy, had some serious marital issues. She tried to placate her husband and ignore or patch the marital problems by continually trying to lose weight, but she was not trying to solve the right problem.

We may think we know this, yet when we place ourselves in this woman's position or face problems in our own
lives, we readily discover solutions that focus on our looks or
bodies. In fact, as you read that story, did you silently decide
for yourself which "solution" you would have chosen, or did
you realize that this woman's problem was not her weight?

We need to consciously remember not to turn all of life's
problems into beauty or weight issues. Don't let other people tell you your problems are caused by beauty problems or,
even worse, tell you that their problems are caused by your
beauty problems as this woman's husband was doing.

The problems we are tempted to ignore are not always as
drastic as marital problems, but they can be equally important in our lives. Don't let yourself delay working for career
advancement or starting a new relationship until you have
lost weight. Don't put your life on hold until you can solve
some beauty problem or finally have plastic surgery. Your life
is your life and your looks are your looks, but the two aren't
necessarily as interdependent as you might think. Telling
yourself you will change or enjoy your life once you look the
way you want to is often a disguised excuse to ignore your
real problems. You don't have to be beautiful to solve your
problems, but you may have to be willing, honest, and brave.

SECTION FOUR

SEEK SELF-ACCEPTANCE

SEEK SELF-ACCEPTANCE

We all want to feel important, loveable, capable, and peaceful. We know that we can go on to do our best in life only after we have made peace with who we are, which includes making peace with our physical selves. It truly is a shame that this is such a hurdle for so many women. Deep inside we know it shouldn't be such a difficult task—but it is. The good news is that self-acceptance is something we can achieve, not in a grasping, if-I-just-work-at-it-hard-enough sense but in a gentle, trusting, open and receptive sense.

In this section on self-acceptance, we examine some mental practices we can use to strongly enhance our own feelings of self-acceptance and inner peace. Perhaps most importantly, you can work on reminding yourself to trust in a Creator for the reason you are who you are. You can remember to be thankful for your health and appreciate your normal healthy appearance.

You must learn to be as positive toward yourself as you are toward the people you love. Focus on your inner life and your strengths and virtues. Have compassion for yourself and others. You can begin to focus on your body with pride, thankfulness, and unselfconsciousness. You can also practice acting as if you had already accomplished your goal of unselfconsciousness.

In this section on self-acceptance, you'll find additional practical suggestions such as seeking therapy for deep or complex problems, avoiding people who have an appearance obsession, and getting to know more inspiring women as role models. You will also learn to accept the admiration and love of people who love you.

As you incorporate a healthy self-acceptance into your way of thinking, you will find new ways of thinking about your true self and your life, ways that are not limited to appearance-based judgments.

53

THERE IS A REASON
WHY YOU ARE WHO YOU ARE

You are beautiful and precious in my sight. (Isaiah 43:4)

You are unique and valuable. If you have lost sight of this because of all the shallow criticisms of a narrow-minded culture obsessed with female packaging, then take comfort in what you know is a larger truth. There is a reason why you are who you are. Call this reason God, Creator, Nature, or Dharma. The truth is simply the truth; it does not matter what name you happen to give it. Trust in this truth. It will give you relief and freedom from continually questioning, doubting, and criticizing your physical body.

Your reason for being who you are, physically as well as spiritually, is not simply "luck" or "genes." Your reason for being here is much larger, and it has nothing to do with the improvements you wish you could make to your body. An omniscient, perfect force wanted you here just as you are. Denying the perfection and wisdom of your own reason for being is denying something much greater than yourself. Feeling that your appearance somehow diminishes your importance is a denial of your humanity and your spiritual worth.

In addition, if you are spending time and emotional energy working hard on your appearance but never spending time discovering your spiritual self, you are putting beauty ahead of spirituality. Your priorities show themselves in what you do, not in what you claim to value.

Focusing on your appearance as a major detraction from your happiness and sense of self is a rejection of the sacred power in you that is meant to work through you. You are so much more than you think.

54

RECLAIM THE
SELF-LOVE YOU HAD AS A CHILD

I absolutely love watching my one-year-old daughter in the bathtub. She is thrilled by the feeling of the water on her body—warm water between her toes, running water splashing off of her fingertips. She examines her little round tummy, pats it approvingly and rubs water on her smooth skin. Barely able to reach her ankles, she rubs her legs with the palms of her hands, enjoying the feeling of skin on skin. Her curly red hair is matted and damp, clinging in wisps to her flushed cheeks until she pats those too with water or bubbles, laughing until she gets water in her eyes. She does not wonder for a fraction of a second what she looks like while enjoying this experience.

I watch in envious reverence. Did I ever feel this comfortable in my skin? Did I ever thrill to the feeling of air and water on my body, delight in a belly because it was my belly, enjoy my legs because I could feel them, see them wiggle?

Yes, there was a time, I tell myself. I felt this bliss as a child. We all felt the delicious, unexamined, tactile sensations of just being when we were children. As infants we never stopped to wonder whether we were good enough or deserving enough to receive pleasure. The comforts of food and warmth, hugs and kisses carried no price tags—no worries about calorie count or jean size. Enjoyment of an activity was not burdened with the compulsion to look good while doing it.

These simple, innocent feelings about our bodies should not have been taken from us. There is no justifiable reason this part of the human experience should have been replaced by self-consciousness, comparisons, and self-loathing. While a return to complete unselfconsciousness would take an immense shift of body awareness unattainable by most of us, we can try to reclaim a small part of this simplicity. As much as possible, we can try to keep in mind this memory of the innocent self-love we were born with.

Whenever possible, give yourself a moment to enjoy the physical sensations of just being alive. Pay attention to tastes and smells and feelings. Savor your food. Close your eyes in the shower and feel the warmth of the water. Take a walk and feel your muscles working. Snuggle under your blankets. Hug someone. Forget about your appearance and remember how wonderful it is to be alive.

55

LEARN TO
APPRECIATE "NORMAL" AGAIN

If you are bemoaning your "beauty flaws," you are most likely wasting time worrying about or disliking features that are perfectly normal. Isn't being normal appreciated anymore? Isn't being normal and healthy enough of a blessing, enough to ask of your body?

The simple truth is that the features or body parts you are unhappy with are most likely normal. Women have been taught to see the world through a fun house mirror where everyone normal looks huge. Every potential normal role model who might be used has been airbrushed out of mass culture. The only real-life role models around you—mothers sisters, friends—seem inadequate and smaller than life and are most likely struggling with the same issues you are. This is sad because real people are the rule, not the exception.

So what is normal/average/healthy? Almost everything fits this description except what you see represented in fashion and advertising.

Normal weight is much heavier and covers a wider range than you have been led to believe. For women, if your waist is relatively smaller than your hips, you are probably at a healthy weight for you. If you eat a variety of foods, do a physical activity three or four times per week, and have kept your weight stable, you are probably at a healthy set point.

There are about five million possible breast shapes and sizes, all of which are normal. Ask your doctor about detecting the signs of breast cancer; those are not normal.

It is normal for your body to change after childbirth and lactation. You may have slightly stretched skin or stretch marks, softer breasts that are less filled out, bigger feet, wider hips. All of these changes are normal.

Aging is normal. If you look a little older than you did last year, it is not because you are weak willed or you don't buy the right creams. It is because you didn't die and are a year older.

Hunger is normal. Eating is not a character flaw; it is the physiologic response to hunger. Hunger and eating are signs of health in a human. Eating feels good. It is necessary and friendly and sane. Make sure you eat a wide variety of healthy foods. It's normal. If you have been eating fake or diet foods or junk food for so long you don't know what healthy foods are, then see a nutritionist or read a book on nutrition.

Remembering to appreciate what is normal and healthy in your body is an essential step toward healthy self-acceptance. Wouldn't it be lovely to someday live in a world where it is normal for women to be satisfied with their bodies?

56

EXPERIENCE YOUR
BODY FROM THE INSIDE OUT

How do you routinely think about yourself? Do you make a habit of being aware at all times of whether you look just right, of wondering how other people see you? Do you find yourself comparing your appearance to an idea of what you should look like? We live in a world that seems to have its eyes on women every spare moment. Sometimes it feels like girl watching is a national obsession—and we can end up doing it ourselves. We can unintentionally go through life watching ourselves or feeling as if the world is watching us, and we experience ourselves in an unnatural way, from the outside in.

What does it mean to experience your body from the outside in? Looking at yourself from the outside is concerning yourself with other people's point of view. "How do I look?" "Do I look silly doing this?" "What do others think of me?" This way of thinking about yourself is uncomfortable, but more important, it limits your experience of yourself. You end up too distracted to focus on your thoughts, feelings, and intentions. You may be too self-conscious to enjoy yourself or do a good job. A woman who is ultraconscious of how she looks limits her consciousness of her inner experience, her thoughts and feelings. It doesn't matter whether she is self-absorbed because she thinks she looks great or because she thinks she looks terrible—she is still concentrating on the experience of herself from the outside. In the ancient Chinese spiritual guide the *Tao te Ching* the philosopher Lao Tse warns, "If you care about people's approval, you will be their prisoner."

When you don't focus on other people's approval you are free again to be yourself. Let go of the need for approval. As Lao Tse explains further:

> *Tao people know themselves,*
> *And make no display,*
> *Accept themselves*
> *And are not arrogant. (Tao 72)*

You can begin to acknowledge your body's inner responses when you live by what you feel and think. How do you feel while taking a walk, enjoying your food, making love? Take time to think, really think, about what you are doing, whom you are with, what is happening around you.

When you feel satisfied and fulfilled by your inner experience of living, you will feel more confident and no longer rely on opinions and approval from others. The result is a feeling of unselfconscious comfort in your self and your body. This is the natural reward for living from your inside out, rather than your outside in.

57

BE COMPASSIONATE TOWARD YOURSELF

Be gentle with yourself. You are not perfect—no one is. Your happiness in life can be greatly enhanced if only you will learn to be compassionate toward yourself. This is true in many areas of life. Being compassionate toward yourself can mean not mentally nagging and berating yourself for your mistakes, not causing yourself mental stress and feelings of failure. It can also mean being patient and humorous with yourself about your body. By being compassionate toward yourself in this way, you can find the patience to care for your health and your appearance in reasonable ways rather than abuse your health trying to achieve unrealistic weight loss or physical changes. With compassion toward yourself, you can react to age and change with humor and grace.

When you can accept your limitations, your needs, and your physical self, you rise above the need for envy, competition, and comparison. Have you ever noticed that the worse you feel about yourself, the more prone you are to envy another beautiful woman? If you feel a need to diet or lose weight, do you ever feel angry at your mate for eating or become overly critical of his weight? If you are unforgiving of your own aging, you may feel resentful toward younger women. By learning compassion for yourself, focusing only on understanding your own body and your own needs, you can stop resenting or comparing.

I have had a hard time learning this principle, but here is an example of a situation when this idea helped me: Each of the four times I was pregnant, it was extremely hard for me to exercise and keep my muscle tone. My breasts were huge, my back hurt, and my joints were like rubber. I returned to my prepregnancy weight eventually, but it was always hard to get back in shape after each baby. My husband, Brett, and I are both casual runners, and it drove me absolutely insane that he kept running while I was pregnant. I wrestled with the envy and resentment I felt because I couldn't stay in shape and he could. There was really no need for me to feel that envy or resentment. He wasn't hurting me by staying in shape; the problem was in my mind. I needed to focus only on understanding myself, not on comparing myself with him. I needed to center my thinking on the self-compassionate idea that "This is my body, and that is all I need to think about. I am happy that I am able to have this baby, and whatever changes I am going through, they are the right changes for me, for my body."

When we learn compassion toward ourselves, it helps us to live without envy, self-criticism, or comparisons. Allow this concept to help you feel more accepting of your body, your appearance, and your physical needs.

58

STAND IN YOUR OWN
ROMANTIC SPOTLIGHT

A friend of mine blurted out that she suddenly was feeling frumpy and middle-aged. She had recently returned from a trip to Costa Rica with her husband. "Ugh. All those thin young women in bikinis on the beach," she shuddered.

For a few minutes my heart sank, too. "I know exactly what you mean," I said. How can we compete with that? There will always be someone younger and prettier.

As I thought about my friend's experience, I reminded myself that we shouldn't be competing because when competition and comparison starts, nobody wins. Whom do you compete with? Do you want to look better than your neighbors and coworkers, better than most of the women on your college campus, better than everyone on a beach you visit? When does the competition stop?

I am not suggesting that we are consciously competing every time we start to feel a little less than glamorous. A better explanation is that we just get distracted from our own specialness because the beauty culture messages around us keep reminding us that anyone with a great body in a bikini is "special."

I thought a little more about my friend. She has been happily married for fifteen years and has two vibrant sons and a husband who adores her. She runs and skis, and she is the kind of person who will sign up for a triathlon for the fun of it. She and her husband visited Costa Rica because they plan to live there for a year. She is learning Spanish for the planned move and will probably return to Alaska fluent in this second language. She is also a musician whose guitar and banjo playing I'm sure will delight her Costa Rican friends and neighbors.

Her life is starting to sound quite romantic, isn't it? "Frumpy" and "middle-aged" aren't terms that fit her. Focusing on the enjoyable features of her life will create for her a unique romantic spotlight should she choose to stand in it and forget about the girls on the beach. This spotlight is the kind of everyday romance in all our lives that deserves celebration.

What is your romantic spotlight? What is special in your life? If your present life is not all you want it to be, then focus on what you aspire to and can do in the future. Build this vision of your own specialness for yourself. Appreciate the people in your life. Look for the beauty in your life. Take time to admire your partner. Be positive and inspire yourself about your present and future. Create your own romantic spotlight. Then stand in it.

59

BE THANKFUL
FOR WHAT YOU HAVE

Someone somewhere is worse off than you are. Look around you and you will see someone who has less to be thankful for than you, someone who has more physical problems or who has not been blessed with your physical health, beauty, strength, or abilities. You will rarely need to look far to find someone less fortunate in some way.

This attitude may sound crude, even cruel at first, but the objective is to help you feel thankful for what you are. In order to stop feeling negative about your appearance, you need to realize how fortunate you are to have the body you have. If, in order to make yourself thankful, you need to see how lucky you are by comparison, do it. This is not reveling in the misfortune of others. It is more like my grandmother's old saying, "There but for the grace of God go I."

If you can't be thankful for your fat-but-functioning thighs, consider the person who can't walk. If you're feeling unlucky about your breast size, consider the woman who is fighting breast cancer. If you're not quite happy with your hair color, remember the people in this world who still can't get penicillin.

The first step of this attitude adjustment is to stop feeling sorry for yourself. It is an unhealthy and unproductive emotion. Self-pity is mostly simple ingratitude—the opposite of thankfulness—for what you do have.

The second, more important, step is to learn to actually use thankfulness. Thankfulness is a powerful tool in building happiness and self-esteem. Thankfulness activates powerful emotional energy that enables you to continue creating more positive thoughts and useful personal energy.

In all honesty, at first I thought thinking this way was pointless. My husband would try to cajole me out of my blue, self-pitying moods. I was not consoled. I still grumbled inwardly about my body issues. I was not experienced in feeling thankful and it didn't come readily.

Self-pity and resentment, on the other hand, I was practiced at. In our youth- and beauty-obsessed culture it is easy to be convinced that being gorgeous, carefree, and young is your birthright. I felt that if I wasn't perfect the world owed me an explanation. Something was wrong if my life didn't look and feel like a diet cola commercial. Right? Wrong.

I was young, and when one is young it can be especially difficult to grasp the fragile gift of daily life and health. When we are more mature we understand more easily how much there is to be thankful for—healthy babies, a loved one's recovery from illness, a nice home, and enough food to eat.

Think about a time in your life when you have been immensely thankful. Remember that warm, powerful sensation of relief, security, happiness, and love all rolled into one. This is a feeling you can evoke over and over about your life, your body, and your health. It is a powerful antidote to self-pity and feelings of inadequacy.

60

ACT AS IF YOU ARE
FINE THE WAY YOU ARE

The philosopher/psychiatrist William James once said, "If there is a quality you wish to possess, act as if you already possessed it." Consider what might happen if you decide to act as if you enjoy your body and feel comfortable with your natural appearance. What if you act as if you were deaf or immune to the pressures of our beauty-obsessed culture? Try it.

Wear the clothes you like, whether they make you look thin or sexy or fashionable or not. Once in a while, don't bother with makeup or your hair.

Eat some really indulgent foods and don't feel guilty, or give yourself permission to feed yourself like a finely tuned athlete, paying almost selfish attention to your nutrition.

Don't wait to achieve some new and improved self before you go on a vacation or a date. Just go and have fun.

Don't feel compelled to apologize for your weight or gray hair. Act as if it doesn't bother you.

While trying out your new approach, it is important to adopt a positive mind-set. Don't make a defiantly negative statement, such as, Okay, fine, I'm a fat slob and I simply don't care what anyone thinks of me. Instead think, I am comfortable with myself and I am going to have a good time. If you are trying to get comfortable going out with minimal makeup and simple hair, don't tell yourself, People are going to see how unattractive I really am. Think instead, I like knowing there is a side to me that is simple and natural.

Two things are very likely to happen. First, you will start to feel better about yourself and start to feel less pressure to look good. You will have started to break the link between your appearance and your enjoyment in life. Second, people will start to see you differently. It is a truth as old as time that people see you the way you see yourself.

Once you start acting comfortable with yourself, you will soon feel comfortable with yourself.

61

THINK ABOUT PEOPLE YOU LOVE FOR THEIR INNER BEAUTY

Think about the people you love. Unless you are an exceedingly shallow person, you do not love them for their looks alone. You love and admire them for who they are inside. You don't love your grandma or your parents or your children for their appearance. You don't choose your friends based on their fashions or figures or drop them if they gain a few pounds or start showing their age. Maybe you were originally attracted to your mate for his looks, but once a real relationship began, you loved him regardless of how he looked.

Interestingly, as you get to know and care for someone, he or she frequently becomes more handsome or beautiful to you. Conversely, we have probably all known someone good looking who is so nasty on the inside that the more you get to know her the less appealing she becomes!

Why do we sometimes find it difficult to give ourselves the same unconsidered, simple acceptance and love we give others?

You know that you can love and be attracted to other people for their personalities, their inner beauty. You know what is important in a relationship and in a person. You are capable of loving and accepting someone else regardless of physical appearance. If you are willing to, you can give yourself the same courtesy.

In addition, you have to trust that other people value you for who you are. You also have to firmly believe that the relationships you have that are based on this kind of acceptance are more important than any applause or admiration, criticism or censure you get based on your appearance.

62

GIVE YOUR BODY
CREDIT FOR PAST PERFORMANCE

Think about something good your body has done for you in your lifetime, something that does not involve appearance. In the search for bodily perfection, women are trained to see their bodies as problems to be solved. We see all the little imperfections as glaring evidence that our bodies are worthless. But our bodies are not worthless, and achieving media-standard perfection does not make them more worthy. We make our bodies worthy through our lives and our troubles and our little triumphs.

Think about your own life, about something you admire about yourself or can credit yourself for, such as recovering from a difficult surgery or having a baby. How ironic that we mothers may be most depressed about our appearances after performing such a miraculous function as giving birth to another human.

Maybe you have always been secretly pleased you are good at some unusual or difficult activity. Maybe you used to be good at a sport and know you could be again. Maybe you have strong hands, good endurance, or great aim with a softball.

You can give yourself credit for surviving adversity, saying, "This body has kept functioning through obesity, bad nutrition, or drug addiction. It may need a tune-up, but at least it is still running!" Surviving hard times gives people character; you can give your body the same credit.

We are conditioned to never praise ourselves for the strength, natural beauty, and functions of our bodies. How often do you hear yourself contradicting a compliment or minimizing congratulations that were given to you sincerely? Many of us were raised with a strong belief that it is improper for girls and women to be self-confident., assertive, or proud. Girls, we were told, shouldn't be "uppity" or "stuck-up." A strong woman may be labeled a "bitch." At the same time we are force-fed a prescription for what we are permitted to take pride in—shiny hair, smooth legs, weight loss. We are encouraged to take pride in battling the natural functions and changes of our bodies and to find fault with ourselves instead of looking for our natural strengths.

It is easy to see how we have lost the basic skill of bolstering our self-esteem about body issues. Look at your body and your life with a new appreciation. Find a way to give your body and yourself credit for performance, not appearance.

63

WANT WHAT YOU HAVE

You are guaranteed to be unhappy if you focus on what you don't have instead of what you have. If you never see the value in your own material possessions, your body, or your life circumstances, then no matter what you attain or what your life is like or how wonderful you may look, you won't enjoy it.

One mental tool you can use to help you appreciate what you have is to ask yourself if you would trade what you have for what you desire. You can mentally compare the worth of the life, family, and health that you have to the exaggerated beauty values and appearance goals you think you want.

For example: Would you trade your eyesight if you could instantly become the most beautiful woman in the world? Would you give up your children and all future fertility to have a perfect, shapely body and remain forever young and gorgeous? Would you agree to die at age fifty if you could be the world's most glamourous woman until then? How about age forty?

You most likely never thought of the intrinsic value of what you already possess. Thinking about giving up or losing valuable parts of your life is a way of regaining perspective. Wanting what you already have is a powerful way to find happiness and contentment in life, a concept that can help you to achieve self-acceptance.

1111111111111111

64

RECOGNIZE WHEN YOU NEED PROFESSIONAL HELP

Seeing your self as a whole and deserving person is an important step in resolving self-esteem and body-image issues. Taking the responsibility to evaluate your life, your self-image, and your emotional health is a critical part of this quest. You may have to do a lot of painful self-examination. But sometimes this task can be too much to take on alone.

Sometimes feeling bad about yourself or worrying excessively about your appearance is an indication you may have deeper problems to deal with. Look within yourself and ask yourself honestly if there are fears, lingering resentments, or emotional scars that you have not resolved. Maybe you have not even recognized them.

Problems with self-image can be closely tied to problems in a marriage or other love relationship. In addition, if you have been abused in any way in the past, those wounds can take a long time to heal and can affect your attitude about your body.

Ignoring deeper issues such as marital or sexual problems or childhood abuse will not make them go away. And your dissatisfied feelings about your appearance will not go away either, no matter how much you improve your appearance.

If you know or suspect that you have an eating disorder, if you ever purposely starve yourself or use vomiting or laxatives to control your weight, you need to see a competent therapist who has experience in treating eating disorders. If you ever feel panicked or controlled by your need to eat, not eat, or lose weight, or if you ever feel seriously depressed about your weight or eating, please see a therapist. You can get your life back, and you deserve to.

If you think your feelings about your appearance are caused by deeper problems or if you think you need help, seek psychological counseling. It is an important, mature, self-affirming act.

65

ACCEPT THE ADMIRATION
OF SOMEONE WHO LOVES YOU

As you are learning to feel more accepting of yourself and your body, be receptive to the admiration and acceptance of those who love you. This includes your husband or lover. Accepting the admiration and attention of your lover sounds like such simplistic advice, but it is often hard to do. Why does a woman so often find herself apologizing about her body to the very man in front of her who is wildly, enthusiastically ready to make love to her? When we feel we have to measure up to the sexualized images of women in the media, it breeds a lot of insecurity in the bedroom. Have you ever heard yourself discounting the opinion of your lover when he says he likes you the way you are? If so, you are definitely not alone; it is a very common problem for women. Contradicting the admiration of your lover becomes a problem for both of you because your insecurity serves not only as a rejection of yourself but also as a rejection of him.

You can stop this habit of deflecting his admiration, rejecting his love and appreciation. You can stop insisting on comparing yourself to idealized body images. You can begin to nurture your self-image by trusting, accepting, and absorbing the love and appreciation that are offered to you.

First, you must stop contradicting him if he offers compliments. Don't dispute it if he says he finds you cute or loveable or pretty. Don't tell him he's crazy; don't point our your

perceived flaws. Don't burden him with the duty of constantly reassuring you. And don't contradict silently either,
telling yourself, What does he know? He just doesn't see how
awful I really look. Just smile and say thank you graciously.
And at least try to believe it. When you learn to become
more receptive to his appreciation, you will begin to accept
the idea that you are a wonderful person and a desirable
lover.

Second, you have to stop comparing yourself to idealized
body images. You are the person this man has chosen to be
with. If what your lover loves about you doesn't seem in your
mind to measure up to the beauty culture ideals, it really
doesn't matter—it is you he loves and wants to be with.
Maybe you should consider that you are the one being shallow and insensitive and bringing the mass market woman
into the bedroom with you, not him. If you feel you need to
be beautiful enough to be the object of universal male desire,
you turn yourself into an object. You don't need to look or
feel like a centerfold model to have a wonderful sex life and
a meaningful relationship and to feel loved. It truly is enough
to have one person who really loves you and the way you
look. But you have to develop the inner self-confidence to
accept his appreciation.

Part of developing that inner self-confidence may mean
you have to cope with your fears. Fear of rejection, fear of
feeling inadequate, and fear that you will lose control or lose
his love or show weakness are all common fears in an intimate relationship. One powerful way to get past these feelings is to label them. When you are feeling a scary emotion,

label it; identify what you are feeling, and then just leave the emotion alone. In other words, if you are feeling lonely or insecure, tell yourself, This is loneliness, or this is insecurity. You don't need to try to "cure" the emotion; just realize what you were feeling, and then try to get on with your life or your relationship. Most often just identifying the emotion helps to clarify the situation and you will feel less controlled by fears and insecurities in a love relationship.

By learning to identify your fears, to stop comparing yourself to other women, and to accept praise and attention, you will be more open to the love and support of another person. Learning to accept the love and admiration of your lover can become for you a powerful source of validation and nurturance and a rewarding, enjoyable improvement in your relationship.

66

DON'T SPEND TIME AROUND OTHERS WITH APPEARANCE OBSESSION

Trying to overcome appearance obsession is like trying to conquer an addiction—it is extremely hard to keep your perspective when you are around other people who are addicted. They undermine your new way of thinking, and old insecurities resurface. If you spend time with others who are on unhealthy diet merry-go-rounds, you will wonder if you shouldn't go back to worrying about your weight, or you will be tempted to do something drastic or unhealthy about your weight. If you spend time around someone in search of perpetual youth, your own wrinkles will seem a little more significant. Don't let others unknowingly keep you convinced of your own supposed inadequacies. You have started this process of affirming your worth and beauty as a person and as a woman. You don't need to hear more beauty propaganda.

I am not suggesting you shun your friends or alienate your family. You can change the subject if appearance, dieting, or similar topics keep surfacing. You might even want to explain your new attitudes. You may be rewarded with more meaningful conversations and deeper relationships.

Also, once you begin to really dissociate your thinking from all the beauty propaganda and obsession, they will start to seem tedious. When you begin to supplant your beauty anxieties with meaningful personal growth, you won't want to return to your old ways of thinking. Feeling fine about your appearance will become second nature—you won't need to discuss plans for continual improvement or confess your beauty flaws. You will start each morning with the grooming products and fashions you love and then forget them as you get on with your day. You will enjoy nutrition and fitness for what they are—one part of a healthy life, not a way to achieve perfect beauty and not a way to prove your worth. You will accept each day for the blessing it is and be thankful also for the blessings of age and the maturity that come with it.

67

FIND REALLY
BEAUTIFUL ROLE MODELS

You want and deserve to find happiness, respect, and love in the body you have. You don't need to be a perfect beauty in order to be happy or successful. Your character, talents, virtues, and spiritual presence are truly what make you interesting, valuable, and beautiful to others. Reaffirming these truths is the basic message of this book. Yet sometimes it can be so hard to believe that these principles could apply to us personally. Finding examples of women whose character overshadows their supposed physical flaws is a helpful way to reassure yourself that you, too, can be defined by your personhood, not your waistline.

It feels encouraging and motivating to be around women who are happy, confident, and beautiful on their own terms. The irresistible strength that comes from not caring what other people think rubs off and is very liberating for women. I am convinced that many women love Rosie O'Donnell because she exemplifies the carefree attitude of liking herself whatever her body weight happens to be. Get to know women who are self-confident and motivated; you can find them in your community participating in the arts, local businesses, or sports.

You can also find many inspiring examples of famous and accomplished women who have succeeded (even in the beauty-obsessed entertainment industry) who do not typify the beauty culture standards. Whatever it is about your body that seems so distressing to you, someone somewhere probably overcame that "flaw" by not worrying about it or even making it her trademark. Find a famous role model who is less than perfect like yourself. Use her example to remind yourself it took personal strength and talent, not just a perfect face and body, to get where she is.

As another example, I have always admired the actress Meryl Streep. Although her looks are probably ordinary by some standards, when she is acting on-screen, she is entrancing. Her expressiveness and her passion make her absolutely luminous. Or consider the great singer Aretha Franklin. When one is watching her it is hard to distinguish whether her beauty comes from having a grand, voluptuous figure or having a soulful, voluptuous voice. Famous women like these make us realize what is most important about them or any woman is not her looks.

We don't have to settle for the mannequin-inspired role models the media reveres—young women chosen for their pretty faces or unusual proportions. How is a role model like that going to improve your life? You can only look at her and feel miserable that you don't look like her. We can and must thoughtfully choose whom we will admire and why. When you find a woman whose talent or intellect or personality is so special that it illuminates her physical presence, that is the kind of person you want to use as a role model. You can't change your appearance to try to look like every beautiful woman around, but you can aspire to improve your character, your talents, or your mind to emulate the women you admire. Look for the "really beautiful" women in your life, and find role models to inspire, motivate, and encourage you to believe in yourself.

68

FIND REAL
WOMEN TO BE WITH

Being around and aware of other women allows us to see ourselves in a more natural context. When we are exposed to only a limited and idealized version of a woman, we may be disheartened by how lacking we seem compared to the ideal. And that ideal is becoming more unreal than ever. In fact, our cultural vision of the perfect woman has become so ludicrously unrealistic that when a recent popular women's magazine presented the "ideal woman" on its cover, she wasn't even a real woman! She was a "cyber chick," a computer-generated composite of ideal female features.

Have we reached some chillingly Orwellian future? Is the only desirable female not only impossibly thin, unrealistically beautiful, airbrushed, and surgically altered but also not even human? Is it any wonder women feel insecure about their bodies?

To be continually exposed to these unrealistic versions of females distorts our thinking. A girl today sees thousands more plasticized two-dimensional images of glamour in a week than her mother did in a year. This situation is not healthy because these images are not real.

Gloria Steinem wrote an interesting article in 1981, "In Praise of Women's Bodies." She describes the satisfying and mind-expanding experience of spending a week exclusively in the company of other women at a health spa. She praised the sisterly experience that developed as the women grew comfortable in each others' presence—clothed, unclothed, trim, chubby, tall, short, young, old. Like her, we can feel the strength that exists in communal femininity. We can also feel the relief of realizing women are just women—diverse, imperfect, human.

Women and girls today have more opportunities to see each other in gyms and health clubs than did women raised in the fifties and sixties. Unfortunately, the discrimination in favor of thin bodies is more firmly enculturated now than ever before. Normal women who are large or who don't fit the aerobic-instructor body image are so stigmatized in our society that many stay away from health clubs, pools, and saunas. The very places where women have the opportunity to share their physical diversity instead end up being microcosms of the beauty culture where only the thin and beautiful dare show themselves.

Paradoxically, our body-obsessed society is opposed to normal, life-affirming exposure of the female body. You can see provocative full frontal nudity at seven in the evening on cable television, but you won't see childbirth. Kids can watch soft-core pornographic music videos after school, but a woman can be asked to leave a restaurant for breastfeeding a baby.

Find ways around this slanted world-view. Spend time doing physical activities with women and girls. Walk with your neighbors. Swim with your daughters. Don't look away when your girlfriend is nursing her baby. Talk to other women in the sauna. Look at them. Look at yourself.

Encourage camaraderie rather than competition in locker rooms and public places where women gather. Find real, live women to be around, and appreciate that you are one of them.

69

APPRECIATE YOURSELF AND
YOU WILL APPRECIATE OTHERS

It is a well-known psychological fact that what we train ourselves to see in the world we will find. Likewise, what we look for in ourselves we will find. If we look for beauty and goodness, whether in ourselves or in others, we will find them. The unique beauty you are learning to look for and appreciate in yourself, you will learn to look for and appreciate in others.

Let me share an interesting experience: As I progressed in the writing of this book, as I watched women, talked to women, read about women, my perceptions changed. I began to see people differently. I believed I already had a healthy love and appreciation for other women. As I continued working with these ideas, though, women around me began to seem very lovely, alive, and individual. Each woman seemed luminous and special.

What was changing? Was it my perceptions of myself? Was my growing understanding of self-acceptance making me more loving toward others? Was my desire to convince women of their own individual worth making me more attuned to people's uniqueness? Was my increasing awareness making me notice other women more?

Probably all of the above were factors. I hope you, too, will experience a new appreciation for other women as well as for yourself.

70

TALK ABOUT IT

Everywhere I go, I listen to women talk about beauty and body image and about wanting to be satisfied with themselves. One fact has become perfectly clear: women talk about these topics all the time. But it is not out of vanity or obsession. In fact, I believe women are beginning to talk about issues of weight and appearance more than ever because they are fed up with society's preoccupation with their looks and their bodies. Women are tired of having their bodies seem like public property—tired of a social etiquette that allows, even encourages, insensitive comments about their weight, their bodies, their age.

I hear many women starting to ask questions. They ask why women are condemned to have so many weight and body image problems, why women live their lives feeling so judged about their appearance. They confront the issue of why women's aging is so abhorred. Some of them wonder why these questions are still around after three decades of feminism.

But the questions and problems are still here, and we need to talk about them. Sharing fears and insecurities about weight, body, and appearance relieves some of the frustration. Making your declaration of personal liberation from the diet war is best done in the rallied, supportive presence of other women who have had the same experiences. Revealing your secret eating disorders and weight struggles deprives these problems of their power to shame. Women are hungry to find they are not alone in the mute frustration of living in a world obsessed with their physical bodies but intolerant of their physical diversity.

Dare to question the meaning of femininity, beauty, and body size in your own life. Discuss these topics openly in the company of other women. Challenge the social stigmas attached to being an aging woman. Talk about the effects of the beauty culture on the lives of women. And listen.

It is immensely gratifying to sit in a coffee shop, as I did recently, and overhear women talk about their long struggles with appearance and body image and to hear stories conclude with personal declarations of independence: "I finally don't care what people think of me. This is what I am. This is what I look like. I feel good. I'm healthy. I'm happy with myself." This conclusion is what we need to talk about. By talking we can shorten the struggle and get to the happy ending more quickly.

SECTION FIVE

ENJOY HEALTHY
SELF-IMPROVEMENT

ENJOY HEALTHY SELF-IMPROVEMENT

The aesthetic appeal of feminine beauty is not going to go away. We certainly don't want it to. Women are lovely, and we deserve to see ourselves that way. Paying attention to our appearance or wanting to improve our physical bodies is good. Of course we should strengthen, explore, and enjoy our physicality and sensuality. Striving for the goal of a healthy mind in a healthy body improves our lives. Our sensual appreciation of beauty in ourselves, in other people, and in the world enriches our lives.

But we do not have to settle for a frustrating obsession with our bodies in order to achieve beauty and health. We can have health and beauty and woman-friendly ideals about both without torturing ourselves. We can become fit for the purpose of longevity and strength, not sexual display. We can enjoy self expression through our appearance. In this final section on healthy self-improvement, we consider some of the many positive ways to accomplish these healthy goals.

For example, when we see ourselves as fully human, physically as well as spiritually, we know we cannot tolerate having our bodies or those of our friends and daughters starved or tortured because of guilt over food. We can reclaim the simplicity of eating.

In addition, we can find our way back to a healthy connection with our female bodies. We can rediscover our deepest instincts, our subconscious strength, and the cyclic rhythms that enrich and characterize our lives as women.

In the quest to grow and improve, we cannot divorce the physical from the spiritual and intellectual. We must seek ways to improve not only our bodies but also our minds, exploring the knowledge that we are beings of mind, body, and spirit. All of these perspectives can combine to help us find healthier means of self-improvement that do not demean or control us but actually help us to live contented, healthy, and beautiful lives.

71

SELF-ACCEPTANCE LEADS
TO HEALTHIER SELF-IMPROVEMENT

Self-acceptance does not mean you will never become any better than you are today. It means you acknowledge you have the strength and inner potential to improve yourself but that you choose to be at peace with what you are and where you are today. In the words of Zen master Thich Nhat Hanh, "The present moment is where life can be found, and if you don't arrive there you miss your appointment with life." You must start with the decision to unconditionally accept yourself today—now. You will never magically recognize a day when you are "improved" enough or thin enough or beautiful enough to be happy with yourself.

When you are at peace with yourself, you will also more clearly see the wasted energy you have been spending trying to achieve an unnecessary and elusive perfection, trying to make changes in yourself that don't really need to be made. You will recognize the difference between improving yourself and mindlessly seeking change. The real change you are seeking is your own approval.

If there are areas of health and fitness or appearance you really do want to improve, you can begin to help yourself by having an open mind and an open heart. Your choices will be much more self-affirming. As you decide on areas you need to work on, you will become more self-confident, knowing you are already "acceptable," and you will not undermine your own efforts with self-doubt and self-criticism. Since you will now credit yourself for your strengths, you will use these without reservation to change your weaknesses. As you learn to respond respectfully and joyfully to your own inner needs, your efforts to improve yourself will become not a punishment but rather a celebration of yourself.

72

KEEP YOUR SELF-RESPECT

All people have their limits, or at least they should. If you have certain personal goals you want to achieve, make sure you can achieve them with dignity and grace. A woman who respects herself as a person should not stoop below the level of her self-respect for the sake of beauty. You can't buy the respect back simply by achieving the beauty goal. If you are trying to become happy with your appearance and learn to appreciate your body, what good is it if you have to violate your larger sense of personhood in order to reach your goals? How can you ultimately be happy with your looks if you have to treat yourself as someone worthless and undeserving in the process?

Here are some examples of processes that may lessen your self-respect: using diet techniques that involve group shame or humiliation; denying yourself the basic rights of eating well, dressing well, or living well until you feel you deserve them; spending money you don't have for diets or beauty treatments; criticizing yourself as a form of motivation.

My personal vendetta is against all the bizarre suggestions for appetite suppression designed to shame women out of eating. You may have seen them in magazines or books of beauty tips:

- Eat your meals wearing only a bikini.
  (What would my kids think?)

- Put an excess amount of salt and pepper on half your food in restaurants so you can't eat it.
  (My husband, who likes to nibble from my plate, would starve.)
- Keep a mirror in your kitchen.
  (Why not just make women eat in the bathroom?)
- Keep ugly pictures of yourself on the refrigerator.
  (Crayon art goes better with my decor.)
- Sniff candy wrappers to kill your cravings for chocolate.
  (Should one hide while doing this?)

These are ridiculous contortions of everyday life. It is probably healthy to resist your cravings for chocolate once in a while, but please don't sniff garbage in order to do it. If these activities help you achieve your appearance goals, what have you traded for them in the process? If you have a goal that you cannot possibly achieve without compromising your personal standards of dignity, without making yourself feel degraded, then maybe you should reconsider that goal.

Self-respect is the most basic validation that allows you to make healthy choices in your life. Self-respect is a reason for maintaining a healthy lifestyle, not the reward for self-denial and self-denigration.

Do what you need to stay healthy and feel beautiful, but be a real person about it. Keep your self-respect.

73

"NOT LEGAL FOR TRADE"

I noticed an interesting detail about my bathroom scale the other day. There were four block–letter words on the dial face: NOT LEGAL FOR TRADE. In business terms, that means it is not legal to determine the commercial value of an item based on the weight measured by that bathroom scale.

We should take that legal advice a bit more personally. It is not reasonable or moral to determine the personal value of a woman based on the numbers on the bathroom scale. Do not buy and sell your sense of self-worth based on that commercially ineligible number. Don't hang your sense of achievement or attractiveness on that fickle little dial. You are a human being. You are too valuable and unique to determine any part of your self-worth by an arbitrary number.

Height, weight, bust/waist/hip measurements, dress size—don't torture yourself with numbers. Women come in more than one beautiful shape and size. It is an unfair manipulation of our ideas about women to believe one weight range or dress size or body measurement is unequivocally more beautiful than any other.

More important, your size, shape, or physical condition definitely has nothing to do with how good a person you are. It is an affront to the human spirit to imply these measurements are related to personal virtues. (Yet that message is implied everywhere you look in our beauty- and-weight-obsessed culture—"There are no ugly women, only lazy ones," said cosmetics mogul Helena Rubenstein.) Weight, shape, and size are physical measurements, not spiritual or psychological measurements. The woman who thinks she has no inner work to do because she is gorgeous on the outside is as painfully deluded as the woman who decides she is weak or a personal failure because she can't lose weight or can't make herself gorgeous on the outside. Both women are selling their souls to the numbers.

You want to be healthy and look well. And if you want to measure your progress, you may need numbers to log the miles you have walked, count your increased repetitions of muscle-toning exercises, or total your servings of vegetables. You should control your blood pressure, cholesterol, and weight in a rational way. Numbers are tools to use when they help you. But remember when it comes to your soul, your sense of personal worth, these numbers are not legal for trade.

74

CONSIDER THE
COST OF PLASTIC SURGERY

When I was a young physician, on a few occasions I was required to administer anesthesia to female patients who underwent plastic surgery in a suburban hospital. Liposuction was a foreign and morbidly fascinating procedure to me. The first time I was involved in the procedure, a twenty-two-year-old woman was scheduled the next morning for her second such surgery. I reviewed the anesthetic requirements of the procedure. I learned that the amount of fat suctioned through a rigid tube reamed under the skin into the fat must be strictly limited and extra intravenous fluids must be administered during the general anesthetic or the woman could go into shock and die or suffer serious major organ damage. This was no minor procedure.

I spoke with the young woman in the pre-operative room the next morning. She was exotic, with dark skin and long auburn hair, and voluptuous, with an average build and a slight plumpness. She was very young, perfectly healthy, and about to have an operation.

Speaking with a Middle Eastern accent, she confirmed this was her second procedure; she had had her hips and belly "done" and now was having her thighs "done."

"I am a dancer in an exotic club. You know all these men," she confided, "they want to see a little bit of leg. You know, they are all pigs."

I was probably not the only woman in the operating room who felt a certain moral queasiness about the procedure on this young woman. I actually regret not having suggested she reconsider (even though I had little authority to do so), especially after hearing the bitterness in her motivations.

Contrast that story with a touching account from a young woman friend of mine who described the breast reduction that relieved years of physical discomfort as well as self-consciousness and embarrassment. She explained to me after having the breast reduction, "I was just always so uncomfortable. My bra straps dug in; I could never run or exercise vigorously. I felt like all anyone could see of me was my breasts. I simply feel a lot better now. I can wear nicer clothes now, too, since I am not covering up so much."

Talking to this friend, I was genuinely happy for her.

Appropriate and life-enhancing opportunities for corrective and cosmetic plastic surgery are available to women, but there are also misogynistic, ethically reprehensible technologies aimed at the remaking of women's bodies to fit a synthetic fantasy. Don't lose sight of the fact that most appearance-enhancing plastic surgeries are performed on women, not men, for "problems" very specific to feminine physiology. No multi-million-dollar surgical industry has sprung up to rescue men from the self-esteem torments of narrow shoulders or small biceps. Think long and hard before undertaking this venture. Don't make a hasty or uninformed decision. Read everything available about the procedure and ask a lot of questions.

If you are considering altering one of your physical features through plastic surgery, it is your decision. If you are otherwise satisfied with your body, plastic surgery may help you to change a feature you just couldn't be satisfied with. It can be a realistic change to help you feel pleased about your appearance. But plastic surgery can also be motivated by frustration or by a desire to achieve unattainable ideals that show a profound disrespect for your body. Please be sure you know the difference.

75

THINK HARD ABOUT WHAT REALLY MAKES YOU FEEL BEAUTIFUL

What we need and want as women is more beauty, not less. But it has to be on our terms. As real people, we want our lives and ourselves to be living works of art. We do not want to be starved, surgically altered, wrapped, squeezed, and painted as passive objects to be critiqued by others.

Reclaiming our souls from the beauty culture does not mean rejecting beauty. It means seeing ourselves and other women through a vision undistorted by the lenses of the beauty culture. It means taking back control of how we want to look and how we want to feel about our bodies, faces, fashions and sexuality.

However, no one can or should dictate any unified prescription for a pro-woman kind of beauty. Striving for the oxymoron of uniform individuality will not solve our problem. No one should tell us to stop shaving our legs or stop wearing makeup or to wear military jumpsuits instead of skirts. Those nonchoices are just as limiting as the prescription to be skinny, white, seventeen years old, and a size six. Our claim must be to decide for ourselves—each woman for herself. But before we claim we have the right to decide, we have to be honest with ourselves about our choices and the motivation for those choices. What we want to do and why we want to do it need to be carefully separated from our training in the beauty culture.

I cannot tell myself I choose to wear high heels because they make me feel good if they actually make my back and feet hurt. If what actually feels good is the stereotypical male attention and a preconditioned feeling that I am projecting a sexual image, then I am not being honest about my choice.

If a large woman chooses to wear a silky flowing gown that does not reveal the shape of her body, I hope she is wearing it because she likes the smooth, luxurious feeling of the gown, not because she feels she must hide her body from the social disapproval.

If you wear lingerie in the bedroom, you owe it to yourself to be honest about whether it enhances your own sensual pleasure or whether it is the gift-wrap on yourself as an object.

If you wear makeup, wear it because it is an artistic expression of yourself and you feel good with it or without it. Wear it the way children love to paint their faces and the way aboriginal people painted the beauty and mystery of nature onto their skin.

In *Celebrating Girls*, Virginia Rutter tells a charming story of a young girl who has received a makeup set for her eighth birthday. Her mother winced, disappointed that her daughter was exposed so young to the role-specific artifice of the beauty culture, but she finally consented to let her daughter put on makeup for that special day. The mom was thrilled a few minutes later when the spirited little girl pranced into the room with half of her face purple, the other half blue. How beautiful!

76

EXPRESS YOURSELF
THROUGH YOUR APPEARANCE

Self-adornment is a highly symbolic act for women. Clothing, jewelry, and face and body cosmetics have probably always been an enjoyable part of womanhood and femininity. It is a richly nourishing act to express yourself through your appearance. It is a sad deprivation to forgo this feminine experience because you are trying to fit standards of appearance that don't suit you. You can completely miss the fun and freedom of dressing to feel nice or to amuse yourself if you feel pressured by appearance standards or because your ideas about how to look feminine have been molded by the beauty myth.

You should not feel you have to wear black because you think you have to look thin when what you really crave are wild prints and flowing blouses. How self-negating it is to always wear sexually provocative clothes because they are the fashion or because you think you must attract men when your heart wants long skirts and lace collars. If strength, seriousness, and respectability are important parts of who you are (even if only in certain situations), show it in your attire.

On the other hand, nothing is wrong with a fashion statement, as long as the statement is coming from you—not dictated to you by the fashion industry. A woman who always looks fashionable but never looks like herself is the real fashion victim.

The way you dress and present yourself expresses a little of who you are, your particular mood that day. The process can also work in reverse—how you dress can influence how you feel and how you behave. You can use this principle to your advantage. You might even be interested in learning about the psychology of color and how it influences your mood.

Convince yourself that you deserve to dress in a way that feels right to you, that helps you to feel competent, relaxed, and interesting. Life is too short to ignore the creative fun of expressing yourself through your appearance. The rules of feminine appearance have become altogether too confining and stereotypical thanks to the beauty culture. You can help yourself and other women to loosen these appearance prescriptions if you make your own individual choices about your dress and appearance.

77

USE YOUR BODY TO ENJOY LIFE

Developing character and intellect is a huge part of a shift in priorities away from our looks and our bodies. But that is not to say we should choose to live sedentary lives only. Our goal is not by any means to deny our physicality; our bodies are, after all, the vehicles in which we live our lives. And most of us women do not complain about the thinness cult and beauty stereotypes because we hate our bodies or hate physical pursuits but because the beauty culture seems to hate our natural bodies.

You should use your body to live your life to the fullest. Many activities can broaden your life experiences and give you more confidence for your self-esteem. These don't have to be physical activities, but if they are, they will remind you that your body is about function as well as form. Physical pursuits can remind you of that blissful feeling of strength, movement, and freedom you may remember from childhood.

For example, take a whitewater raft trip. Travel somewhere you have always wanted to go. Learn a new sport. (It doesn't have to be javelin throwing; it could be as simple as a community t'ai chi class.) Be brave. In fact, dare to look stupid once in a while—it's good for you. And the next time you are at a party, instead of considering your looks, you will be telling people about your Himalayan experiences or the principles of aikido.

The point of these activities is not to change your shape or improve your fitness, it is simply to make your adrenaline flow. These activities can make you feel powerful and confident. Even if you already consider yourself a confident person, there is always some new adventure or skill you haven't tried; you can keep getting better! Besides, more women participating in sports and community activities breaks the ice for other women. Take a friend.

Take an active role in your community. Volunteer to help fix a local trail or playground. Join Habitat for Humanity and you can literally help to build a house for someone who desperately needs one. Thinking about other people, volunteering, and serving your community is an incredibly powerful way to be less self-absorbed.

Another way to enjoy life is to explore your creativity. Forget all the brainwashing you've heard that only some people are talented. We are all talented, all creative. Find a creative activity you would like to try and do it. Take lessons or trade lessons with a friend—for example, you can teach her piano; she can teach you oil painting. If you think you would enjoy some artistic activity, try it. What harm can it do? You might have a lot of fun. It will be one more skill, talent, or hobby that is not beauty weighted. Just think, when you are seventy, you may be wrinkly or a little pudgy, but you will have a gallery full of beautiful oil paintings or pottery to show off.

The mass market woman, on the other hand, is only pretty. She never has a hair out of place, she never stinks when she sweats, she never looks inept because she never tries anything more adventurous than a new hair color. She can't waste time helping others because she is too busy with her looks. She does not become more interesting, vital, and creative with the passing of time.

You are not that woman. Get involved. Serve others. Achieve large or small physical feats and learn new skills. Explore your creativity. All of these are great ways to broaden your sense of yourself and improve your life, not just your looks.

78

LET REAL LIFE
MAKE YOUR BEAUTY DECISIONS

If you wanted to present yourself at all times in your most polished, optimum beauty, you could spend all day trying. I have known someone like this. It literally took her three to four hours to prepare herself for a day, and she spent a few more hours on touch-ups and freshening through the day. She was very unhappy, and I have never met a shallower person.

You can pay any price you are willing to for your beauty. You can pay in time, money, self-consciousness, and effort. The price is almost limitless. Luckily for most of us, real life has a habit of getting in the way. Real life is more than willing to give you advice on what kind of beauty commitments are reasonable, optional, or out of the question for you.

For example, with four small children, I spend a lot of time cleaning house, changing diapers, scraping peanut butter off walls, and of course, washing my hands. As a physician, I have spent plenty of time wearing irritating latex gloves and, again, washing. I admire nicely groomed hands with nail polish and smooth skin. Realistically, though, I'm lucky to find time to use a nail clipper once a week and hand lotion once a day. I am satisfied with simple hand grooming because it is my choice, based realistically on my life.

Real life also involves money. Be realistic about your finances. If you are going broke in order to keep up your beauty image, maybe you should re-evaluate your priorities.

Pay the rent first. If you refuse to buy expensive clothes, products, or beauty services so that you can pay your other bills, then you are allocating your money wisely. You should be proud of your common sense, not embarrassed about your image.

These are not compromises you should feel distressed about. Remember, you are making these choices. You should feel important and in control of these beauty decisions. Your time is important and so is your money. Money, time, health, peace of mind are the currency of your life. Free yourself to make reality-based appearance decisions without feeling unfeminine, inferior, or inadequate. It is your business, your life, and you are in control.

79

TAKE CARE
OF YOUR BODY

A healthy mind and a healthy body are your goals. You can set your sights above and beyond the capricious standards of ideal beauty. Refuse to be seduced away from your goal of real health by the lure of just looking healthy. What beauty industries convince women to do for "natural beauty" is usually far from natural or healthy.

Instead, find out what you need to do to be truly healthy. Inform yourself about women's health issues. Find out what your own real health risks and history are. Stop smoking. Follow healthy nutritional guidelines; maybe treat yourself to a visit to a nutritionist. Find a good doctor. Get your mammograms and pap smears on schedule. Learn how to perform a careful breast self-exam, then examine yourself monthly. Make informed decisions about birth control; practice safe sex with someone who loves you. Don't ever put up with being hit, hurt, or harassed by anyone. Inform yourself about hormone replacement therapy if you are menopausal. Avoid purposely tanning your skin. Have unusual moles checked by a doctor. Use sunscreens. Find exercises and physical activities you can love and use them to rejuvenate your body and mind.

Take care of yourself. Glorify in the body and life and health you have now, while you have it. Care for your health—it is a beautiful gift.

80

USE PHYSICAL ACTIVITY TO
FEEL BETTER ABOUT YOURSELF

Your quest is to feel better about yourself. More important, it is for you to feel better about yourself exactly as
you are. You don't need to lose weight, firm up, tone, or
beautify. But physical activity in itself can make you feel
remarkably better about yourself.

It is not through strengthening or firming that this
process works. It works because your body is meant for
movement. Movement increases the circulation of oxygen
everywhere in your body, including your brain. The endor-
phins produced in your brain are natural antidepressants and
make your body crave movement to produce these chemicals again. Your body will appreciate a chance to breathe
deeply, your heart to beat, your muscles to stretch, and your
mind to relax.

If you are not used to moving or exercising, consult with
a doctor first and start slowly. Be sure to find an activity you
love. And always pay attention to whether the exercise is
making you feel good. Don't "go for the burn," and don't
work through pain.

If you are an avid exerciser, but working out sometimes
feels like punishment and doesn't leave you feeling good, try
slowing down and enjoying gentle movement. Use gentle
movement and an enjoyable activity to break the habit of
using exercise as a punishing way to force your body to

change. Avoid the kind of exercise that requires mindless, painful repetitions. Use exercise that nourishes your body and mind. Instead, enjoy the scenery and the time to reflect or have fun.

Whatever your relationship to body and movement has been to this point, consider this: walking is magic. Meditative walking is probably the most ancient and effective exercise for one's body and mind there is. Walking is just you and the earth and the air. The rhythm of the human stride is a calming chant from body to mind. Experience this rhythm of connection between muscle and spirit and breath. Do it every day if you can. Use physical exercise in the natural way it was intended—as a method of strengthening mind, body, and spirit. Feel how it improves your sense of well-being.

81

EAT SOMETHING

For goodness' sake, eat something. That's right, feed yourself. The beauty culture and its obsession with thinness has too many women believing they don't actually deserve to eat. Choosing to eat only healthy foods is fine, but literally feeling guilty because you ate when you were hungry is lunacy. Women have been made ashamed to eat food—real food. They have been convinced they must not indulge in food so they can make themselves thinner and smaller—until they disappear entirely. If the beauty culture has specifically defined a beautiful, desirable female body as one that does not eat, then by sick extension of this logic, the best, most desirable female is a dead anorexic.

Reclaim the right to sustenance, nourishment, and pleasure through food. Commit the act most often forbidden to women by the beauty culture. Commit the act of conscious self-feeding. Make it intentional, purposeful, and enjoyable. After all, in every other context, eating is an act of love and nurturance, community, and social acceptance. Break bread with yourself, with a loved one, with your family, with other women.

Eating in this way is an act of rebellion. It proclaims your belief that what is female is not made worthwhile only by being starved, neglected, slenderized, weakened, or in any other way minimized. Instead, what is female deserves to be strengthened, nourished, nurtured, fortified.

Our thinness–obsessed society has turned food and eating completely inside out for women. Eating is not an act of weakness, it is an act of strength! Eating was not meant to make people feel miserable. Food should not invoke guilt. Food is nourishment. We would not have so many weight problems if the diet industry had not turned food into such an emotional issue.

Fearing that you will "lose control" over your appetite and your body is not the real problem. If you are dieting or restricting your natural healthy eating patterns trying, hoping to fit the ideal body type, then you are not the one in control of your appetite or your body. You may feel shame, anxiety, or guilt. You may have a compulsion to feel beautiful and admired or a fear of the derision our society reserves only for fat people. But it is not you who has control over your need to eat. The beauty culture does.

You will have control when your urge to eat does not make you feel anxious, guilty, or anything other than hungry. You will have control when the desire for companionable breaking of bread or the comfort of a warm cup and a full belly seem to you like a completely reasonable part of the human experience for women, as well as men. So eat something. Consciously, thankfully, joyfully.

82

RELEASE CONSCIOUS CONTROL;
ALLOW SUBCONSCIOUS SELF-CARE

Every person is naturally equipped with a powerful instrument for maintaining health and well-being. It is your subconscious mind. Your body-mind duo is meant to take care of you. Your subconscious mind plays an important role in achieving goals that you consciously decide on. If you have ever had the experience of being so focused on achieving a goal you didn't even need to think about how to achieve it, you have seen subconscious programming at work. You may have experienced this in sports or when preparing for an extremely difficult exam. When you are subconsciously directed, self-discipline becomes a nonissue. Motivation is completely internalized.

Your subconscious mind also affects your well-being—illness versus health, vitality versus fatigue. Do not continually try to control and restrict your daily life—struggling with your appearance, your appetite, your activity, and your energy. Do not restrain your natural urges to eat or drink. Do not continually think about your appearance and how to change it. When you continually inflict these self-conscious limitations on yourself, you unintentionally handicap the powerful unconscious energies that can make your life joyful and effortless, your appearance natural and healthy. Your subconscious mind, when healthfully nurtured and allowed to function, can guide you into more healthful, creative, and self-loving habits. You have only to trust yourself, and trust nature.

You can eat and drink when you are hungry and thirsty without fear of unhealthy weight problems. Your body and inner mind can work in partnership to find your healthy set-point. You will recognize your basic drive to be physically active. You will crave fresh air, movement, freedom, and strength. As an added benefit, your creative energies will begin to blossom. You will enjoy your appearance as an expression of your genuine self. You will find new passion and enjoyment as your internal reserves of joy are tapped.

All of these positive effects arise as you cease your conscious struggles to control your body and allow the natural, health-seeking instincts of your subconscious mind to emerge.

83

RESPECT YOUR
ANIMAL INSTINCTS

"Animal instincts" is really a misnomer. The deep, simple instincts we women (and men) have regarding life and sensuality, pleasure and pain are not animal instincts; they are our very human instincts. Our instincts and appetites for food, sex, solitude, company, affection, excitement, and love are our birthright.

In each of us is a sacred life force that does not abide by the terms and limitations of social rules. At its most elemental, this force in us does not acknowledge the criticisms and compulsions of a culture that says we must look "a certain way" before we deserve to indulge any of these instincts.

Thankfully, our deepest inner selves are wise enough not to let any of those instinctual urges die. Guilt, shame, and feelings of inadequacy are the inhibitors we may feel from an overdose of beauty propaganda, but they are not as deep and powerful as the instincts they mask.

Dare to throw off the suffocating inhibitions and reclaim your human instincts—as many women are doing.

Large women are reclaiming their sensuality and sexuality, which is a great relief to the men who have loved large women all along. Mature women are leading fulfilled, adventurous, meaningful lives complete with love and plenty of sex. The skin cream ads may imply that life and love end at forty, but these older women are simply too polite or too busy to set the record straight. Adult women who have experienced the deeply satisfying female experiences of marriage, pregnancy, childbirth, and breastfeeding realize they are profoundly sexual beings. Pop culture may insinuate that exciting sex is reserved for the young, busty, and carefree, but no one seems to be having sex as much as seasoned married couples.

And sexuality is not the only or even the most important of your instincts. You must eat for pleasure and for sustenance. You must move, breathe, and experience your body and your surroundings as well as find challenge, exertion, and reward. You must involve other people in your life and yourself in theirs. Look for spiritual connection, trust, and love and give them to others. And you must pray and meditate and be alone. Respect your instincts to create and express yourself and find out who you are.

84

GET COMFORTABLE
WITH YOUR CYCLES

Nature is cyclic, changing with the phases of the moon, the seasons, the days. As women, we are blessed to be part of this cyclic harmony. As our bodies follow a monthly cycle of change, we learn to recognize and adapt to our own natural rhythms. Our hormones flux, accompanied by changes in skin, breasts, emotions, and weight. Our cycles and changes are part of nature, neither good nor bad.

Being in harmony with your cyclic self is a part of loving and accepting your body. It can start with the simple act of paying attention. Pay attention to where you are in your cycle; learn about what is happening to your body during each phase of the month. Chart your symptoms on a calendar for a few months to become familiar with your patterns. Recognize the changes and feelings you experience during your cycle.

Even if you have fairly difficult menstrual periods, knowing when to expect changes and being able to understand yourself and your feelings can help. The more in tune you are with your body, the less distressing it seems when your body, constantly changing, doesn't fit the plastic molds of beauty ideals day after day. Once you give up trying to fit a mold, natural changes feel normal.

Why should you worry about a change in your weight once a month when water retention is a natural part of your cycle? Why should you suffer from a particularly low self-image once a month when you could come to the realization that all you need is a little time alone or some extra emotional support at that time?

Getting comfortable with your cycles is helpful in maintaining a balance between your emotional self and your physical self.

85

RESPECT THE
DIFFERENT STAGES OF YOUR LIFE

In the teachings of yoga tradition, life is divided into four phases. In each phase a person encounters different challenges and opportunities for growth. First is the "student," or learning, stage. We all start out not knowing much. Second is the "householder," or nest-building, stage of responsibilities and caring for family or business. After that comes the third stage, called the "forest-dweller," or self-fulfillment, stage, during which domestic or career responsibilities are reduced and a focus on the self is possible. The fourth stage is that of the "wandering scholar," when one naturally seeks a deeper level of spiritual enlightenment and serves as a mentor to others.

Why is this model of life relevant to the issues women face about their lives and their bodies? A model like this is useful to us because so many modern, commercial values about women insist that we deny the physical changes of age, resent the physical demands of a woman's life cycle, or struggle to achieve some kind of artificial sex appeal. We need instead to cultivate an attitude toward our lives and our bodies that allows us to appreciate the beauty and complexity of our lives and to feel accepting of our bodies in every stage.

In a woman's student phase, usually her teen years, mass media and social pressures about sex, slenderness, and appearance can distort her earliest understanding of womanhood and sexuality. Early sexual experiences, eating disorders, and poor self-image are the sad results. We should look back at our own teen years to try to understand where our own ideas and self-concept were formed.

In the nest-building stage of motherhood and career, a woman finds more challenges to her self-concept. During the emotionally monumental and physically demanding phase of pregnancy, childbirth, and motherhood, many women become discouraged because their bodies no longer match the cultural concept of sexiness. However, we can choose to accept the changes that our bodies experience during this stage of life. We can choose to see motherhood as important and precious, not just an interruption in our weight loss plans. And instead of worrying about our bodies, we should focus on the incredible emotional growth this phase of life demands of us.

Next, as a woman matures into the self-fulfillment phase of later adulthood, the demands of family subside. Her career may be firmly established or in a demanding state of flux. In this stage, the shallow values of mass culture can continue to be misleading. We are faced with the challenge to continue finding fulfillment in life, yet the beauty culture advertises that self-fulfillment is about age-defying lotions, liposuction, or maybe a sexual fling.

During every stage of life we are continually challenged to decide which values we will live by—our own or the ones we see in the media. If we recognize the wisdom of a tradition that honors the phases of our lives, we can appreciate and accept the changes of our bodies and appearance. We may even live our lives a little more thoughtfully.

86

EXERCISE
YOUR MIND

If you are spending more time on your body than on developing your mind and continuing your education, you are making a big mistake. The simple fact is you need to exercise your mind. What good is being beautiful if you are ignorant?

Time erodes all physical beauty. The workings of your mind can continue to improve throughout your life. In fact, some studies now show that people who continue to exercise their minds vigorously as they age can delay the onset of age-related senility, just as physical exercise in old age can delay the onset of age-related loss of muscle mass and flexibility.

You can't improve your standard of living by improving your looks. You can by improving your mind. Consider women in low-paying jobs who spend an hour or more a day on their looks. If they took some of that hour and that energy and used it for career advancement, they might be pleasantly amazed by the results. Some women think they are very fulfilled by all the attention physical beauty can bring. "What is the point," they ask, "of reading a book or learning a second language when looking great can get you so much?" The answer is obvious—you don't get that attention forever.

Endlessly cultivating or struggling for beauty gives nothing back to the world and leaves you with nothing more to offer the world than your decorativeness. The wisdom you cultivate increases your ability to contribute to the universe. What you do with your mind enriches us all. Women need to learn from each other. The girls of the next generation don't need you to be cute; they need you to be wise. I would like to learn from you what you have learned about love, motherhood, finance, Japanese art, marine biology, political philosophy, or God. I don't care what your hair looks like.

Improving your mind can make you happy and light-hearted and full of dreams. You can read books and travel and talk to interesting people the way you dreamed of doing when you were a little girl. Embolden your spirit. Discover new thoughts, new places, a new self. Find your passions and interests and sail away on them. When did a diet ever make you feel that good?

No matter what the beauty culture would have you believe, men do love women for their minds. Men are spiritual beings who gravitate to spiritual strength. Men are intellectual beings ready to share intellectual interests. Men are sexual beings, and the brain has always been the most important sexual organ. Men are human beings with hearts and bodies and minds—just like women.

Experimenting with your interests and talents is a way of finding your way to your true self. Experimenting with your appearance is fun, but it does not teach you who you are. Discovering you are a little bit of a redhead at heart is not the same as discovering the musician in your soul or finding you have a head for business. Explore your mind as a way to find your true potential.

87

SELF-IMPROVEMENT SHOULD
NOT CAUSE EMOTIONAL DISTRESS

Beautiful body and weight loss ads combined with the phenomenon of supermodel worship and a national obsession with weight loss can make us feel downright desperate to change ourselves. We have distressing evidence of just how desperate women are about appearance when we read about eating disorders and drastic weight loss surgeries or starvation diets causing medical problems or even death. This undeserved desperation is why we have focused so much in this book on understanding our motivations and seeking self-acceptance.

We still want to live our lives comfortably and healthfully in our bodies, we want to enjoy feeling and looking good, and we may want or need to improve our bodies. The challenge is to find emotionally and physically healthy ways to do this.

You may sometimes need to watch what you eat. You may need to improve your cardiovascular fitness or want to adapt your body to the changes of age.

When you are deciding on a self-improvement method or goal, keep these very important questions in mind: Does it pass your own "emotional distress test"? Does your proposed program or personal change actually make you feel worse about yourself? Does it make you feel deprived, insulted, or frustrated? If an activity doesn't make you feel better, avoid it. There are so many options, different ways to incorporate healthy habits into your life, that there is no need for you to lock yourself into a method or program that doesn't suit you practically or emotionally. Find a way of maintaining or improving your physical health that doesn't harm your emotional health.

If you were tormented in gym class in high school, you may really hate organized exercise classes. If so, don't force yourself to struggle through an aerobics class. Your subconscious will certainly find excuses for you to quit. Rather than force yourself into emotional compliance, find some form of exercise that makes you feel good emotionally as well as physically. When I was a pre-teen I started, unnecessarily of course, to diet stringently. Every aspect of eating and not eating became exquisitely painful. I counted every calorie, every bite. This meant no more hot dogs or toasted marshmallows for me at our lake cabin campfires during the long Michigan summers. This was a very sad and painful way for a thirteen-year-old to deprive herself of the innocent pleasures of childhood eating, but the terrors of the beauty culture loomed larger.

As an adult now, I am less fearful about my body and its appearance. I occasionally have to check on my eating habits to maintain a healthy weight; I may skip dessert or watch my intake of fats once in a while, but emotional distress is off limits. I don't go on diets because they make me too worried about my eating for me to eat rationally. Dieting makes me feel terrible (and besides, diets don't work in the long run), so if I need to get my weight down I would much rather exercise more than feel deprived of food. In addition, there is no lure of slenderness that could compel me to miss the chance to join my kids in eating toasted marshmallows. It is a symbolic deprivation I simply refuse to re-experience.

Do this for yourself: Decide what you want or need to do to maintain your health, achieve fitness or other physical goals, or improve your appearance in enjoyable ways. But do not, DO NOT venture into the arena of emotional distress for the sake of beauty or appearance improvement.

Stand by your marshmallows.

CONCLUSION

In our visual consumer culture, the bodies of women and girls bear an unprecedented level of public exposure and private scrutiny. Women are faced with a potent double-edged sword: rigorous and often unrealistic standards of beauty coupled with an insistent media-reinforced sense of the importance of appearance and the expectation of sexual display. As a result, women and girls today are burdened with a self-consciousness about their bodies that is so deeply ingrained we may find it difficult to question its importance.

We sneer at the idea of women a century ago imprisoned in corsets, yet we hardly recognize how controlled we are by our modern product-oriented ideas about the shaping, starving, and remaking of our bodies. We celebrate the advances made in the lives of women in the past few decades, yet examining our mass culture we see the lives of women insistently directed toward laborious grooming, dieting, and exercising, sometimes at the expense of exercising our newfound freedoms and living meaningful lives.

If we have internalized the idea that we do not deserve fairness, respect, or appreciation unless we look "like a woman should," then we will try to change our looks rather than insist on being treated fairly. If we are desperately seeking the approval of others, then we will not make self-respecting decisions in our lives about our sexuality, equality in the workplace, or our health or safety, to name a few examples. We must solicit our own approval.

The social changes, such as changes in advertising, entertainment, or public opinion, that might improve how women grow up feeling about themselves will not happen unless we change how we think and feel about ourselves today. This was part of the reason I chose such a personal, even emotional approach to the material in this book and the reason for a format that allows us to absorb and reflect on this thinking in small increments.

Equally important, though, whether or not we succeed in changing social attitudes about the importance of appearance, is that each of our lives is special. We each have ideas, feelings, dreams, and abilities, but far too many of our feminine gifts are being senselessly ignored or undervalued or never allowed to flourish, supplanted by the draining agenda of weight loss or beauty improvement or, more tragically, undermined by a mass market notion that our worth as women lies in being merely decorative.

This has been the goal of my book: to help each of us reclaim a way of thinking about ourselves that helps us to feel satisfied with our bodies, yet inspired to improve our lives; to enjoy beauty and health, but in a context that is healthy, realistic, and life affirming; and to search for what is good and inspiring and beautiful in ourselves and other people, but to remember we will not find it on the outside.

We want to live in a world in which women are respected, appreciated, and loved. We want our daughters to grow up feeling rich in their femininity and eager to enter a womanhood that is untainted by the frustrations of appearance prejudice and sexual objectification. We want to enjoy growing into wise, happy old women unconcerned about our bodies and our wrinkles, knowing we carry the secrets of life safe in our hearts. But a world in which women feel freed from undue concerns about their appearance must start with an idea in our own minds and a belief in our hearts. Let us start today to welcome all women into that world.

SUGGESTED READING

On Women, Beauty, and the Media

Brumberg, Joan. *The Body Project*. New York: Random House, 1997.

Douglas, Susan. *Where the Girls Are*. New York: Random House, 1994.

Lehrman, Karen, *The Lipstick Proviso*. New York: Anchor, 1997.

Poulton, Terry. *No Fat Chicks*. Secaucus, N.J.: Birch Lane Press, 1997.

Wolf, Naomi. *The Beauty Myth*. New York: William Morrow, 1991; reprint, New York: Anchor Books, 1992.

On Eating, Weight, and Eating Disorders

Chernin, Kim. *The Obsession*. New York: HarperCollins, 1981.

Orbach, Susie. *Fat Is A Feminist Issue*. New York: Galahad, 1997.

Pipher, Mary, Ph.D., *Hunger Pains*, New York: Random House, 1995.

On Women, Their Lives, and Their Bodies

Beck, Martha, Ph.D. *The Breaking Point*. New York: Random House, 1997.

Hunter, Brenda, Ph.D. *In the Company of Women*. Sisters, Ore.: Questar, 1994.

Hay, Louise. *Empowering Women*. Carlsbad, Calif.: Hay House, 1997.

Martz, Sandra, ed. *I Am Becoming the Woman I've Wanted*. Watsonville, Calif.: Papier-Mache, 1994.

Martz, Sandra, ed. *If I Had My Life to Live Over I Would Pick More Daisies.* Watsonville, Calif.: Papier Mache, 1992.

On Positive Thinking

Carnegie, Dale. *How to Stop Worrying and Start Living.* New York: Pocket Books, 1984.

Martorano, Joseph, M.D., and Kildahl, John, Ph.D. *Beyond Negative Thinking.* New York: Insight Books, 1989.

Peale, Norman Vincent. *The Power of Positive Thinking.* New York: Ballantine, 1956.

On Philosophy

Frankl, Viktor. *Man's Search for Meaning.* New York: Simon and Schuster, 1984.

Dreher, Diane. *The Tao of Inner Peace.* New York: HarperCollins, 1990.

Emerson, Ralph Waldo. *Self-Reliance.* New York: Penguin Books, 1982.

Maslow, Abraham. *The Further Reaches of Human Nature.* New York: Penguin, 1976

Mitchell, Stephen, trans. *Tao te Ching.* New York: HarperCollins, 1988.

On Living, Dreaming, and Growing

Cameron, Julia. *The Artist's Way.* New York: Tarcher Putnam, 1992.

Visit the Mass Market Woman Website

for more information:

www.massmarketwoman.com

207

Date: 11/7/14

GRA 741.5 GRE V.4
Venditti, Robert,
Green Lantern. Dark Days /

GREEN LANTERN

VOLUME 4 DARK DAYS

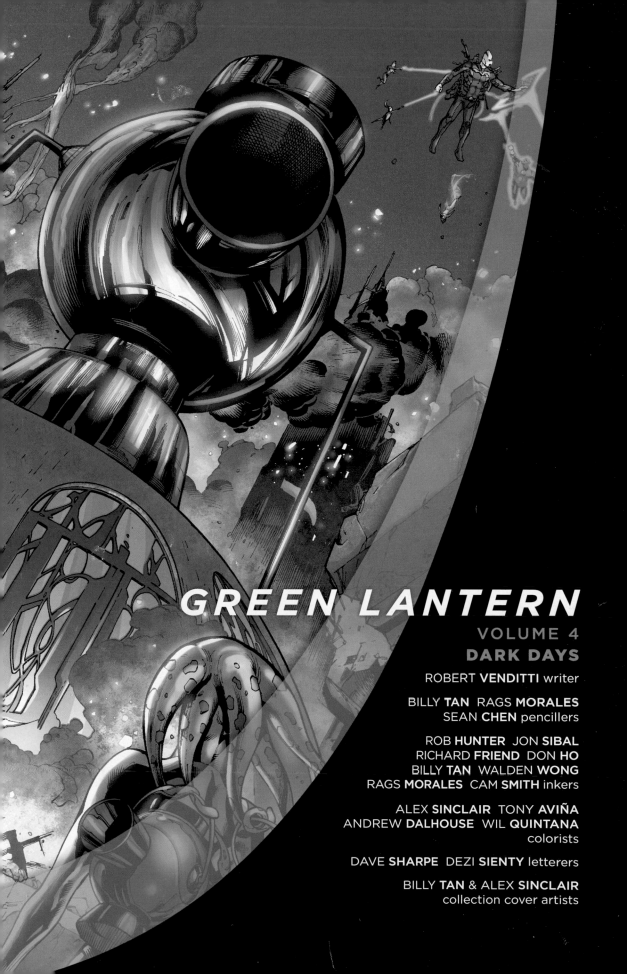

GREEN LANTERN

VOLUME 4
DARK DAYS

ROBERT **VENDITTI** writer

BILLY **TAN** RAGS **MORALES**
SEAN **CHEN** pencillers

ROB **HUNTER** JON **SIBAL**
RICHARD **FRIEND** DON **HO**
BILLY **TAN** WALDEN **WONG**
RAGS **MORALES** CAM **SMITH** inkers

ALEX **SINCLAIR** TONY **AVIÑA**
ANDREW **DALHOUSE** WIL **QUINTANA**
colorists

DAVE **SHARPE** DEZI **SIENTY** letterers

BILLY **TAN** & ALEX **SINCLAIR**
collection cover artists

MATT IDELSON Editor – Original Series CHRIS CONROY Associate Editor – Original Series RACHEL PINNELAS Editor
ROBBIN BROSTERMAN Design Director – Books ROBBIE BIEDERMAN Publication Design

BOB HARRAS Senior VP – Editor-in-Chief, DC Comics

DIANE NELSON President DAN DIDIO and JIM LEE Co-Publishers
GEOFF JOHNS Chief Creative Officer
JOHN ROOD Executive VP – Sales, Marketing and Business Development
AMY GENKINS Senior VP – Business and Legal Affairs NAIRI GARDINER Senior VP – Finance
JEFF BOISON VP – Publishing Planning MARK CHIARELLO VP – Art Direction and Design
JOHN CUNNINGHAM VP – Marketing TERRI CUNNINGHAM VP – Editorial Administration
ALISON GILL Senior VP – Manufacturing and Operations
HANK KANALZ Senior VP – Vertigo and Integrated Publishing JAY KOGAN VP – Business and Legal Affairs, Publishing
JACK MAHAN VP – Business Affairs, Talent NICK NAPOLITANO VP – Manufacturing Administration
SUE POHJA VP – Book Sales COURTNEY SIMMONS Senior VP – Publicity
BOB WAYNE Senior VP – Sales

GREEN LANTERN VOLUME 4: DARK DAYS

DC Comics, 1700 Broadway, New York, NY 10019
A Warner Bros. Entertainment Company.
Printed by RR Donnelley, Salem, VA, USA. 3/21/14. First Printing.

HC ISBN: 978-1-4012-4744-7
SC ISBN: 978-1-4012-4942-7

SUSTAINABLE FORESTRY INITIATIVE

Certified Chain of Custody
At Least 20% Certified Forest Content
www.sfiprogram.org
SFI-01042
APPLIES TO TEXT STOCK ONLY

Library of Congress Cataloging-in-Publication Data

Venditti, Robert, author.
Green Lantern. Volume 4, Dark Days / Robert Venditti ; illustrated by Billy Tan.
pages cm
ISBN 978-1-4012-4744-7 (hardback)
1. Graphic novels. I. Tan, Billy, illustrator. II. Title. III. Title: Dark Days.
PN6728.G74V46 2014
741.5′973—dc23

ROBERT VENDITTI writer BILLY TAN penciller RICHARD FRIEND inker
cover art by BILLY TAN & ALEX SINCLAIR

POWER LEVEL 27%.

POWER LEVEL 24%.

POWER LEVEL 16%.

POWER LEVEL 19%.

RING STATUS: GREEN LANTERN OF SECTOR 3276 DECEASED.

SCANNING SECTOR 3276 FOR REPLACEMENT SENTIENT.

DAMN.

NO ONE ELSE DIES! YOU HEAR ME? WE'RE GETTING *THROUGH* THIS!

FIND A BATTERY WITH SOME JUICE AND *CHARGE UP!*

THEY'RE EMPTY, HAL. *ALL* OF THEM.

ANY IDEAS, SALAAK? HOW WOULD THE *PROTOCOL BOOK* SUGGEST WE HANDLE THIS?

THE CENTRAL POWER BATTERY. IT'S OUR ONLY HOPE.

ALL RIGHT. SALAAK AND JOHN, YOU'RE ON COVER.

NEMUX! TWO-SIX! GRAB AS MANY LANTERNS AS YOU CAN CARRY.

DON'T LOOK SO GLUM, MS. FERRIS.

YOUR *NUMBER ONE* TEST PILOT IS BACK.

AND READY FOR ACTION.

YOU *AREN'T* MY NUMBER ONE TEST PILOT.

TO SATISFY THAT CRITERION, YOU'D NEED TO SHOW UP FOR WORK AND, YOU KNOW, *FLY A PLANE* ONCE IN A WHILE.

YOU'RE PRETTY MUCH JUST A BOYFRIEND NOW. AN *ABSENTEE* ONE AT THAT.

ABSENCE MAKES THE HEART GROW FONDER.

NOW COME HERE, AND LET YOUR *BOYFRIEND* GET HIS HANDS ON--

HAL...

I RECOGNIZE THAT "HAL..."

THAT'S THE "HAL..." YOU GIVE ME WHEN I'VE SCREWED UP.

DON'T.

WHATEVER YOU'RE MAD ABOUT, I HAVE NO DOUBT I DID IT. AND I'M SORRY.

NOW CAN WE SKIP AHEAD TO THE PART WHERE YOU GIVE ME ANOTHER CHANCE, AND WE GO TO DINNER AND A MOVIE?

NOT THIS TIME.

THIS IS A *RING* THING, ISN'T IT?

YES. BUT IT ISN'T YOUR RING THAT'S THE PROBLEM.

IT'S *MINE*.

OUR RINGS TAP INTO THE ENERGY OF THE EMOTIONAL SPECTRUM. YOURS IS FUELED BY *WILLPOWER*--

--AND LORD KNOWS, YOU'RE ABOUT AS WILLFUL AS THEY COME.

BUT I'M A STAR SAPPHIRE. FOR ME TO WIELD THE VIOLET LIGHT, I NEED TO FEEL THE INTENSITY OF *GREAT LOVE*.

YOU'RE SAYING...YOU DON'T LOVE ME ANYMORE?

IF I DIDN'T--

--I WOULDN'T BE ABLE TO DO *THIS*.

I *DO* LOVE YOU, HAL, AND I NEED TO HANG ON TO THAT LOVE WITH EVERYTHING I'VE GOT.

THAT'S THE PROBLEM.

BECAUSE YOU'RE MAKING IT VERY *VERY* DIFFICULT.

WHERE'S THIS COMING FROM? JUST THE OTHER DAY YOU WERE HAPPY TO SEE ME BACK.

OF COURSE I WAS. YOU WERE BACK FROM THE *DEAD*. HAPPY YOU'RE ALIVE ISN'T THE SAME AS HAPPY ABOUT *EVERYTHING*.

I KNOW WHAT IT MEANS TO WEAR A RING. I UNDERSTAND THE RISKS. THIS ISN'T ABOUT THAT.

THIS IS ABOUT WHEN WE *AREN'T* WEARING THEM. WHEN WILL YOU REALIZE LIFE ISN'T JUST BARREL ROLLS AND TECHNICOLOR LIGHT FIGHTS?

THERE *IS* A WAY TO BALANCE BEING A LANTERN AND BEING A PERSON.

FOR CRYING OUT LOUD, YOU'RE A *GROWN MAN*, AND YOU'RE STILL SLEEPING ON YOUR LITTLE BROTHER'S SOFA.

IS *THAT* ALL THIS IS ABOUT? YOU'RE MAD I GOT EVICTED FROM MY OLD PLACE. I'LL GET A NEW ONE.

SOON AS I FIND TIME TO GO APARTMENT HUNTING.

I'M NOT MAD. I'M... *TIRED*.

TIRED OF GIVING YOU SECOND AND THIRD AND *TWENTIETH* CHANCES. EVENTUALLY THERE'S GOING TO BE A *LAST* CHANCE.

AND YOU'LL MESS THAT UP, TOO. I CAN'T TAKE THE DISAPPOINTMENTS ANYMORE. THE ONLY WAY I CAN GO ON LOVING YOU IS IF I'M NOT *WITH* YOU.

WHO KNOWS...MAYBE I *DON'T* LOVE YOU. MAYBE I JUST LOVE THE *PROMISE* OF YOU. WHATEVER IT IS, I CAN'T RISK LOSING IT.

BECAUSE IF I DO, I'LL LOSE BEING A STAR SAPPHIRE. I WON'T LET THAT HAPPEN.

CAROL, PLEASE...

LANTERN JORDAN OF SECTOR 2814: REPORT TO OA IMMEDIATELY FOR BRIEFING.

DUTY CALLS.

I'M SORRY, HAL. WEARERS DON'T CHOOSE THEIR RINGS; RINGS CHOOSE THEIR WEARERS. ALL WE CAN DO IS FIND A WAY TO LIVE WITH IT.

WE'LL WORK THINGS OUT. YOU'LL SEE.

I WISH I HAD YOUR CONFIDENCE. BUT WHO DOES?

RIGHT NOW I JUST NEED SOME TIME APART. SO GO--

THAT WAS *EXHILARATING!*

FOR *YOU,* MAYBE...

YOU ASKED TO SEE ME, GUARDIANS?

JUST A HEADS-UP--I ALREADY RECEIVED MY SCOLDING FOR TODAY.

WE HAVE NO INTENTION OF REPRIMANDING YOU, LANTERN JORDAN. WE WISH TO *PROMOTE* YOU.

YOU ARE THE NEW CORPS LEADER.

EFFECTIVE IMMEDIATELY.

YOU'VE BEEN LOCKED IN A BOX FOR *BILLIONS* OF YEARS, SO LET ME CLEAR UP ANY MISCONCEPTIONS YOU HAVE ABOUT ME.

I WAS BOOTED FROM THE AIR FORCE FOR *DECKING* MY SUPERIOR OFFICER.

TRUST ME, I'M NOT LEADERSHIP MATERIAL.

WHAT HE SAID.

THE PRIOR YEARS' CONFLICTS HAVE TAKEN A *SEVERE* TOLL ON THE CORPS' RANKS.

OUR PREDECESSORS ARE DEAD. MOST OF THE SENIOR LANTERNS LIE IN THE *CRYPT.* BUT NOT YOU.

YOU FACED THOSE BATTLES AND SURVIVED.

INDEED, YOU WERE INSTRUMENTAL IN *WINNING* THEM. AND YOUR FELLOW LANTERNS HOLD YOU IN HIGH REGARD BECAUSE OF IT.

YEAH...YOU'RE OVERESTIMATING THE LEVEL OF REGARD.

ASK ANY LANTERN, AND THEY'LL SAY HAL WAS INSTRUMENTAL IN *CAUSING* A FEW CONFLICTS, TOO. EVER HEARD OF *PARALLAX?*

DO ME A FAVOR? STOP TAKING MY SIDE.

WHAT ABOUT YOU? LEADERSHIP IS SUPPOSED TO BE *YOUR* JOB.

AS YOU SAY, WE HAVE BEEN "LOCKED IN A BOX" FOR TOO LONG.

BEFORE WE CAN *GOVERN*, WE MUST *LEARN.*

IN SO DOING, PERHAPS WE CAN REGAIN THE TRUST THAT WAS *ABUSED* BY THOSE WHO CAME BEFORE US.

THE RESPONSIBILITY OF REBUILDING THE CORPS IS YOURS.

LANTERN SALAAK HAS *RESIGNED* HIS POST AS PROTOCOL OFFICER. LANTERN KILOWOG WILL ASSIST YOU IN HIS STEAD.

WE WILL BE DEPARTING OA.

THIS IS A *PRECARIOUS* TIME, LANTERN JORDAN. HOLD THE CORPS TOGETHER IN OUR ABSENCE. NO MATTER THE COST.

YOU ARE *DISMISSED.*

STAY, LANTERN RAYNER.

THERE IS *ANOTHER* MATTER WE WISH TO DISCUSS...

SAY IT AIN'T TRUE, JORDAN. TELL ME THEY DIDN'T GO THROUGH WITH IT.

AFRAID SO, KILOWOG. THE GUARDIANS ARE LEAVING. NO TELLING WHEN THEY'LL BE BACK.

IN THE MEANTIME, I'M THE NEW *BOSS.*

THE RINGS OF THE FALLEN. JUST WHEN I THINK I CAN'T FEEL ANY WORSE... SO *MANY.*

I SAY WE SEND THEM OUT FOR NEW RECRUITS. MIGHT DO US GOOD TO SEE SOME FRESH FACES AROUND HERE.

WHERE WE GONNA TRAIN THEM? OUR FACILITIES ARE A *WRECK.* FIRST ITEM ON THE TO-DO LIST IS SHORING UP OUR INFRASTRUCTURE.

AND FINDING ME A CHAIR I CAN ⁓GNRF⁓ FIT IN.

I SEE YOUR POINT. BESIDES, IF I'M GOING TO BE A LEADER, I NEED TO BE LESS IMPULSIVE.

HAVE TO *CRAWL* BEFORE I *FLY,* RIGHT?

CONTAINMENT FIELD DEACTIVATED.

SCANNING SECTOR 2387 FOR REPLACEMENT SENTIENT.

SCANNING SECTOR 0916 FOR REPLACEMENT SENTIENT.

SCANNING SECTOR 1122 FOR REPLACEMENT SENTIENT.

ALL LANTERNS TO THE SKIES--

GRUNT LARFLEEZE COULD'VE FIGURED OUT HOW TO MESS WITH OUR BATTERIES...

POWER LEVEL 100%.

POWER LEVEL 100%.

POWER LEVEL 100%.

POWER LEVEL 100%.

WARDEN VOZ, SHOULDN'T SOMEONE KEEP WATCH OVER THE PRISONERS?

YOU WANT THE *BABYSITTER'S* JOB, COSSITE? IT'S YOURS.

THE REST OF YOU ARE WITH ME!

RATHER THAN JOIN THE OTHER LANTERNS, YOU STAY BEHIND AND KEEP US *CRIMINALS* SAFE?

NOT THE CRIMINALS, NOL-ANJ.

JUST YOU.

ROBERT VENDITTI writer BILLY TAN penciller ROB HUNTER & JON SIBAL inkers
cover art by BILLY TAN & ALEX SINCLAIR

OoO...I'VE NEVER SEEN GREEN LANTERNS LIKE *YOU* BEFORE.

YOU'LL MAKE GOOD ADDITIONS TO MY *MENAGERIE!*

AGENT ORANGE AVARICE

SPACE SECTOR ZERO.

OR. CENTRAL PRECINCT OF THE INTERGALACTIC POLICE FORCE KNOWN AS THE GREEN LANTERN CORPS.

KILL! TAKE!

LARFLEEZE WANTS!

ARE YOU FOUR JUST GOING TO *STAND* THERE--

GREEN LANTERN WILL

BOOOOOOOOOOM

IT SOUNDS LIKE YOUR FRIENDS COULD USE YOUR HELP, COSSITE.

I CAN'T ABANDON MY POST, NOL-ANJ. I *WON'T*.

IF THEY BREAK THROUGH TO THE SCIENCELLS, I'LL *DIE* BEFORE I LET THEM TOUCH YOU.

DON'T YOU SEE? THIS IS OUR CHANCE.

HOW LONG HAVE WE BEEN PERMITTED TO ONLY *LOOK* AT EACH OTHER? SO CLOSE IN DISTANCE, YET ALWAYS APART...

WE CAN LEAVE *TOGETHER* NOW. THE CONFUSION OUTSIDE WILL COVER OUR ESCAPE.

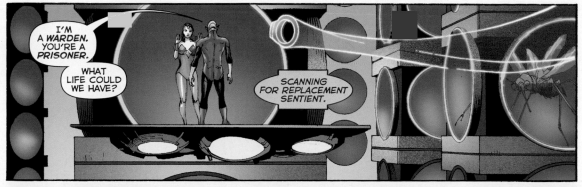

THE RINGS... THEY CAN'T BE MISLED.

IT HAD TO BE DRAWN HERE BY...YOUR LOVE.

LOVE...

I AM CAPABLE OF GIVING GREAT LOVE. BUT NOT TO YOU.

NOT TO ANY *ONE* BEING.

MY LOVE IS FOR MY *CLANN.*

THE CLANN WHO ASKED ONLY FOR MY LOYALTY, AND GAVE ME LOYALTY IN RETURN.

THE CLANN WHO TOOK ME IN WHEN I HAD *NOTHING* AND MADE ME A QUEEN.

PLEASE...

NOL-ANJ...

IT'S TIME THEIR QUEEN RETURNED TO THEM.

THEY JUST KEEP COMING!

STINGY AS LARFLEEZE IS, YOU'D THINK HE'D SPEND HIS LIGHT A LITTLE MORE CONSERVATIVELY.

HNNN--

--NYAA!

NICE ONES, RECRUIT.

I'M BEGINNING TO UNDERSTAND. IT'S AN IDENTITY. AN EQUATION WITH AN INFINITE NUMBER OF POSSIBLE SOLUTIONS.

YEAH, WELL, DON'T GO GETTING TOO CONFIDENT YET.

KILOWOG! GET BACK TO YOUR POST! FIND SOME WAY TO GET US AN UPPER HAND!

YOU AIN'T *GROUNDING* ME, JORDAN.

I GOT TOO MUCH AGGRESSION TO SIT BEHIND SALAAK'S SCREENS.

THEY AREN'T *MY* SCREENS ANYMORE, LANTERN KILOWOG. PROTOCOL OFFICER IS *YOUR* RESPONSIBILITY NOW.

GROUNDED...

THE *IMPOUND HANGAR!* KILOWOG, OVERRIDE THE DOCKING CLAMPS ON ALL THE CONFISCATED *SHIPS.* REMOTE-LAUNCH *EVERY LAST ONE* OF THEM.

THAT'S AN *ORDER!*

WHATEVER YOU SAY, "CORPS LEADER."

BUT IF MY *AMPLE FANNY* LANDS IN FRONT OF A *REVIEW BOARD* OVER THIS, I'M SAYNG *YOU* MADE ME DO IT.

OKAY, WHERE AM I SENDING THESE THINGS?

ANYWHERE THAT ISN'T *HERE!*

"KILOWOG, DID YOU GET THE TREASURE LOADED?"

CONTACT THE ZAMARONS. MAKE SURE THE BODY GETS RETURNED TO HER PEOPLE.

WHAT DO WE DO NOW?

WHEN THE RINGS BROUGHT US HERE, THEY SAID WE WERE SUPPOSED TO REPORT TO TRAINING.

COSSITE...?

WE HAVE A FUNERAL OF OUR OWN TO TEND TO.

YOU WANT TRAINING, RECRUIT? HERE'S YOUR FIRST LESSON. DON'T END UP LIKE THIS.

OF EVERYONE, I FIGURED HE'D BE THE SAFEST.

WHEN THE REST OF THE WARDENS JOINED THE FIGHT, HE STAYED BEHIND TO GUARD THE SCIENCELLS.

YOU DON'T MEAN...

THAT'S EXACTLY WHAT I MEAN.

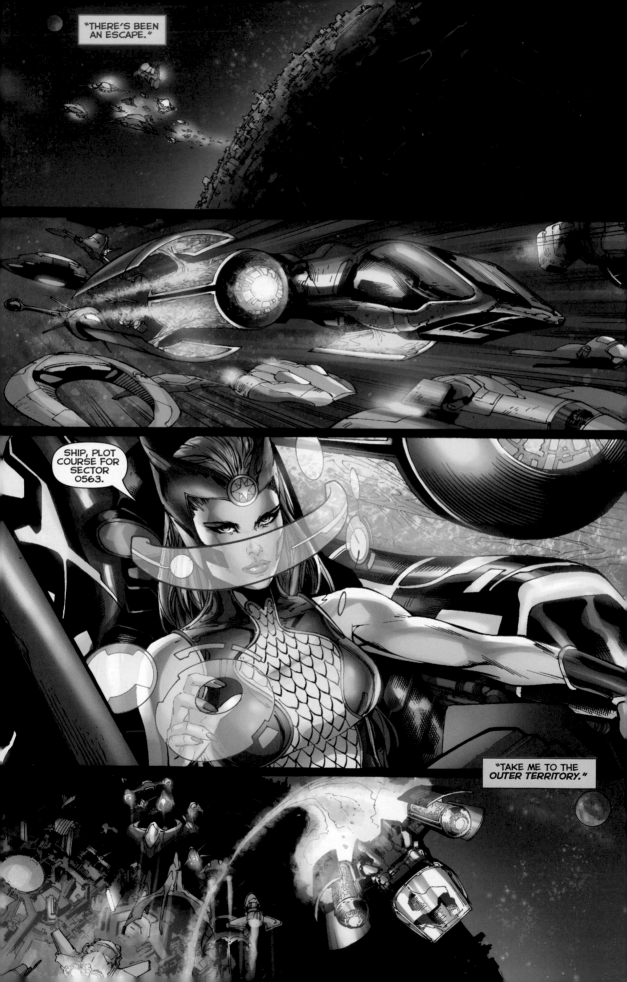

ROBERT VENDITTI writer BILLY TAN penciller ROB HUNTER inker
cover art by BILLY TAN & ALEX SINCLAIR

"SHE NEEDS TO SEE YOU."

THERE WAS NOTHING I COULD DO, HAL.

THEY FOUND HIM BURIED UNDER WHAT'S LEFT OF THE MESS HALL.

ARE THOSE...?

BITE MARKS. LARFLEEZE'S PETS MUST'VE BEEN GNAWING ON HIM WHEN THE BUILDING COLLAPSED.

LARFLEEZE KILLS A STAR SAPPHIRE.

WE LOSE LANTERN COSSITE IN A PRISON BREAK. NOW *THIS.*

WHO IS HE?

I DON'T KNOW. NO ONE DOES.

A RING BROUGHT HIM HERE FROM *SOMEPLACE.* DOESN'T IT HAVE A RECORD?

SURE, BUT *WHICH* RING? NEW LANTERNS ARE STILL ARRIVING FROM SECTORS ALL OVER THE UNIVERSE.

THIS ONE PROBABLY DIED DURING THE ATTACK.

HIS RING LEFT TO FIND A REPLACEMENT BEFORE ANYONE KNEW HE WAS HERE.

SOMEONE TELL ME THIS FALLEN LANTERN'S NAME.

NOW.

HAL, MAYBE YOU SHOULD CALM--

RING, IDENTIFY.

SUBJECT IS VILGASHIAN.

VILGASHIAN? BUT THEY...

CURRENTLY RESIDE ON SEVENTEEN WORLDS ACROSS FOUR SECTORS.

TOTAL ESTIMATED POPULATION: TWO HUNDRED BILLION.

KLANK

HAL?

LIKE SITTING →GRNT← ON A THIMBLE.

GIVE ME SOME GOOD NEWS, KILOWOG. WHAT DO WE KNOW ABOUT THE ESCAPED PRISONER?

NOT MUCH...

PRIXIAM NOL-ANJ. ARRESTED ON THE OUTER RIM OF SECTOR 0563.

NOT SURE IF SHE'S A LOCAL, OR THAT'S JUST WHERE SHE SETS UP SHOP.

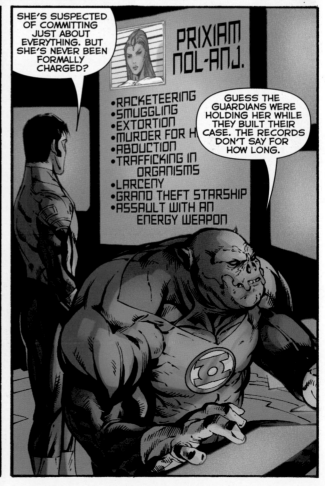

SHE'S SUSPECTED OF COMMITTING JUST ABOUT EVERYTHING. BUT SHE'S NEVER BEEN FORMALLY CHARGED?

PRIXIAM NOL-ANJ.

• RACKETEERING
• SMUGGLING
• EXTORTION
• MURDER FOR H
• ABDUCTION
• TRAFFICKING IN ORGANISMS
• LARCENY
• GRAND THEFT STARSHIP
• ASSAULT WITH AN ENERGY WEAPON

GUESS THE GUARDIANS WERE HOLDING HER WHILE THEY BUILT THEIR CASE. THE RECORDS DON'T SAY FOR HOW LONG.

HE DIED BEFORE HE COULD TELL ANYONE HIS NAME. WE DON'T EVEN KNOW WHERE TO SEND HIS *BODY.*

YOU WANT US TO BE A CORPS? ACT LIKE YOU'RE PART OF ONE.

IF YOU WON'T UPHOLD THE GROUP IDEAL, YOU CAN'T EXPECT OTHERS TO.

IS THAT THE KIND OF CORPS WE WANT TO BE? ONE THAT ENLISTS LANTERNS JUST SO THEY CAN GET *MOWED DOWN?*

HOW LONG YOU THINK RECRUITS WILL LAST IF THEY BELIEVE IT'S S.O.P. TO TAKE DOWN THREATS ON THEIR OWN?

YOU'RE THE NEW CORPS LEADER, AND YOU HAVEN'T EVEN ADDRESSED THE GROUP YET.

MOST OF THEM PROBABLY HAVE *NO CLUE* THERE'S BEEN A LEADERSHIP CHANGE.

SEND A MEMO TO EVERYONE'S RING. POST A SIGN IN THE BREAK ROOM. I DON'T CARE.

BUT I *AM* CORPS LEADER. AND AS LONG AS THAT'S THE CASE, I'LL BE FIRST IN HARM'S WAY.

THE *ONLY* ONE IN HARM'S WAY, IF I HAVE ANYTHING TO SAY ABOUT IT.

FINE LEADER HE'S SHAPING UP TO BE. →SNORT←

EEP!

CRASH

CRK-SNAP

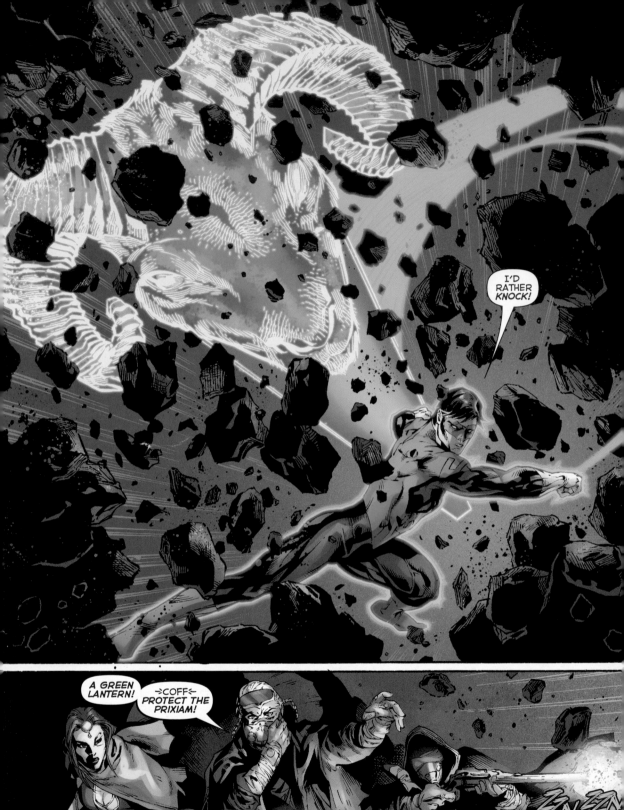

YOU'LL ARREST *NO ONE,* LANTERN.

YOU'RE A ⇒NNG⇐ *STAR SAPPHIRE?*

THE RING FOUND ME IN MY *SCIENCELL.* IT SAID I WAS CAPABLE OF GREAT LOVE. AND I AM.

LOVE FOR MY *CLANN,* WHICH GREEN LANTERN GORIN-SUNN SEPARATED ME FROM FAR TOO LONG AGO.

SIX YEARS IMPRISONED WITHOUT TRIAL. ALL THE WHILE I KNEW MY CLANN WAS SUFFERING.

LOVE?

WHUNK

I'VE SWORN OFF THE STUFF.

CAROL...

THAT DOESN'T SOUND PROMISING.

HOW DOES IT FEEL TO BE *KEPT* FROM THOSE YOU LOVE, GREEN LANTERN?

SYSTEM MALFUNCTION.

SYSTEM MALFUNCTION.

→AGK←

RIGHT. →COFF←

RINGS HAVE BEEN →COFF← *ACTING UP* LATELY.

→GLLK←

BREATHE, PRIXIAM!

→ACK← GULK←

MMPF

ROBERT VENDITTI writer RAGS MORALES penciller CAM SMITH with RAGS MORALES inkers
cover art by BILLY TAN & ALEX SINCLAIR

LONG AGO.

THE EXISTENCE BEFORE OURS.

A WONDROUS DISPLAY.

DAZZLING LIGHT OF EVERY HUE CAST AGAINST THE BLACK, UNBLEMISHED CANVAS OF SPACE.

FROM A DISTANCE, YOU MIGHT INTERPRET THE BURSTS AND STREAKS AS PART OF SOME **COSMIC CELEBRATION.**

OR THE DELICATE **BALLET** OF PRISM BEETLES PIROUETTING BENEATH THE OCEANS OF EVENDON PRIME.

YOU WOULD NEVER IMAGINE THAT WHAT YOU WERE WITNESSING--

--WAS DEATH.

IT DID
NOT HAVE
TO END.

HE HAD TRIED
TO WARN THE
LIGHTSMITHS.

AT TIMES THEY
WARRED TOGETHER
AGAINST A
COMMON ENEMY.

OTHER TIMES THEY
TURNED THEIR WARS
UPON THEMSELVES.

WHATEVER THE
REASON, THE EFFECT
WAS THE SAME.

THE FUEL OF ALL
EXISTENCE WAS
BEING DEPLETED.

THE LIGHTSMITHS NEVER AGREED WHICH WERE THE FIRST TO HARNESS THE POWER OF THE EMOTIONAL SPECTRUM.

IT MATTERED NOT WHO STARTED IT. WHAT MATTERED WAS THAT THE HARNESSING HAD BEGUN.

USING ENORMOUS CONVERTERS, THE LIGHTSMITHS ABSORBED THE EMOTIONAL ENERGY OF THE UNIVERSE AND TRANSFORMED IT INTO POWER.

POWER CHANNELED THROUGH THEIR WEAPONS AND RENDERED INTO THE SEVEN VISIBLE LIGHTS.

HE CALLED THE LIGHTSMITHS TOGETHER ON NEUTRAL GROUND, AND THEY CAME. SUCH WAS THE DEPTH OF THEIR RESPECT FOR HIS SCIENTIFIC ACUMEN.

HE EXPLAINED THE LIGHT THEY WIELDED SO WANTONLY WAS A **RESOURCE**, AND NO MATTER HOW INFINITE IT SEEMED, IT ORIGINATED FROM SOMEPLACE, AS ALL RESOURCES MUST.

AND THE RESERVOIR COULD BE **EMPTIED**. WHAT THEN?

FOR THE LIGHT WASN'T MERELY A DISTILLATION OF EMOTION INTO ENERGY, AS THEY HAD LONG BELIEVED. IT WAS THE ESSENCE OF **EXISTENCE** ITSELF.

WAS NOT GRAVITY SIMPLY ONE OBJECT'S **PASSION** TO BE NEAR ANOTHER?

...NOT EVEN THE BASEST ...E FORMS PERSEVERE ...CAUSE OF EMOTION?

DESIRE FOR WHAT THEY HAD. **TERROR** OF LOSING IT. **FURY** TOWARD THE **GLUTTONY** OF OTHERS WHO SOUGHT TO TAKE IT.

WASN'T SURVIVAL NOTHING MORE THAN A VAST EXERCISE OF **RESOLVE**?

THE UNIVERSE COULD NOT BE ROBBED OF SUCH THINGS WITHOUT A GREAT COST TO BE PAID BY ALL.

NO ONE LISTENED.

HE TRAVELED THE UNIVERSE, SEARCHING EVERY PLANET AND SYSTEM FOR THE RESERVOIR.

HIS ODYSSEY TOOK HIM TO THE FAR-FLUNG EDGE OF SPACE, WHERE HE DISCOVERED A VAST WALL THAT ENCIRCLED THE UNIVERSE AND COULD NOT BE TRAVERSED.

ANYTHING THAT TOUCHED THE WALL BECAME IRREVERSIBLY FUSED TO IT. HE COULD GO NO FARTHER.

WITH NOWHERE LEFT TO SEARCH, EVEN HE BEGAN TO DOUBT THE RESERVOIR'S EXISTENCE.

IF ONLY THAT DOUBT HAD PROVED CORRECT...

THE LIGHTSMITHS CALLED THE EVENT "THE DIMMING."

IT BEGAN ON THE PLANET AXYLUND, PARADISE OF THE BLUE LIGHTSMITHS.

FOR EONS THEIR CONVERTER HAD DISTILLED FAITH INTO AZURE LIGHT, ENABLING THEM TO SPREAD THEIR TEACHINGS AMONG THE GALAXIES.

NOW, THE CONVERTER WAS DARK.

THAT WAS WHEN THE ONE THEY CALLED "RELIC" KNEW HE HAD BEEN CORRECT ALL ALONG. AND THAT ALL WAS LOST.

THE LIFELESS CONVERTER INSPIRED A MOMENT OF PAUSE AMONG LIGHTSMITHS OF EVERY COLOR--

HE WAITED FOR THE
END TO CONSUME HIM.

THE GREAT, IMPASSABLE WALL AT THE EDGE OF THE UNIVERSE CRUMBLED.

FROM BEYOND POURED OUT DARKNESS.

EMPTINESS.

ALL CREATION COLLAPSED TOWARD THE VOID.

HAD HE FOUND THE LOCATION OF THE RESERVOIR HE HAD SO LONG SOUGHT? WAS THE WALL A BARRIER BEYOND WHICH STOOD THE SOURCE OF ALL EXISTENCE?

FOREVER A SCIENTIST, WHAT ELSE COULD HE DO BUT PASS THROUGH?

IF THIS WAS HIS FINAL MOMENT, THEN HE WOULD FILL IT WITH DISCOVERY.

THEN THE
UNEXPECTED
HAPPENED.

HE WAS RE-FORMED AS
PART OF A **NEW** EXISTENCE.

REORGANIZED.

REMADE.

NO LONGER A RELIC
IN NAME ONLY, BUT BY
DEFINITION AS WELL.

THE ONLY SURVIVING
ARTIFACT FROM A **VERSION**
OF **CREATION** THAT WOULD
NEVER BE KNOWN AGAIN.

BILLIONS OF
YEARS PASSED.

HE BECAME SOMETHING A
SCIENTIFIC MIND SUCH AS
HIS COULD ONLY *DREAM*
OF ENCOUNTERING: THE
EMBODIMENT OF AN
EXTINCT AGE.

BUT THE TRANSFORMATION
LEFT HIM INERT, ISOLATED WITHIN
AN ANOMALY IN SPACE-TIME.

A DISCOVERY FOR
THE BEINGS OF THIS
NEW UNIVERSE TO
DECIPHER.

INQUISITIVE
BEINGS.

BEINGS IN *AWE* OF THE
VAST UNIVERSE THEY
WERE ONLY BEGINNING
TO EXPLORE.

BEINGS DRIVEN BY
CURIOSITY TO ASK
QUESTIONS AND
SEEK ANSWERS.

CURIOSITY,
THE ENGINEER
OF PROGRESS...

...AND DESTRUCTION.

SENSING THE PRESENCE OF A LIGHTSMITH, RELIC STIRRED WITHIN THE ANOMALY.

HE HAD TRIED TO REASON WITH THE LIGHTSMITHS OF HIS UNIVERSE. TO CONVINCE THEM THROUGH SCIENCE AND DEBATE.

BUT THEY UNDERSTOOD ONLY **VIOLENCE.**

SO WITH VIOLENCE HE WOULD TAKE HIS ARGUMENT TO THE LIGHTSMITHS OF THIS NEW UNIVERSE, AND HE WOULD NOT STOP UNTIL EVERY LAST ONE OF THEM WAS SNUFFED OUT.

HE WOULD END THEIR CYCLE OF DECAY AND RESCUE CREATION FROM THE WANTONNESS OF THOSE WHO WOULD DESTROY IT. IT WAS HIS CALLING.

WITH THOSE THOUGHTS--

ROBERT VENDITTI writer BILLY TAN penciller ROB HUNTER inker
cover art by BILLY TAN & ALEX SINCLAIR

TOTAL MEANS *TOTAL*, HAL. THE RINGS WENT DOWN *HERE*, TOO.

GOOD THING KILOWOG HAD ISSUED AN ORDER GROUNDING ALL LANTERNS.

SUFFOCATING IN THE VACUUM OF SPACE IS NO WAY TO GET SNUFFED.

THE BATTERY APPEARS TO BE STABLE NOW, THOUGH IT IS OPERATING AT A SEVERELY DIMINISHED CAPACITY.

MY BEST ASSESSMENT IS THAT *ION* WAS THE CAUSE OF THE RINGS' ERRATIC BEHAVIOR.

ION? WHAT DOES THE GREEN ENTITY HAVE TO DO WITH ANY OF THIS?

THAT'S WHAT WE'VE BEEN TRYING TO FIGURE OUT.

JUST BEFORE YOU GOT BACK--

"--THE CENTRAL BATTERY BARFED OUT ION LIKE IT WAS BAD SUSHI.

"SOMETHING WAS WRONG WITH IT. IT LOOKED...*ILL*."

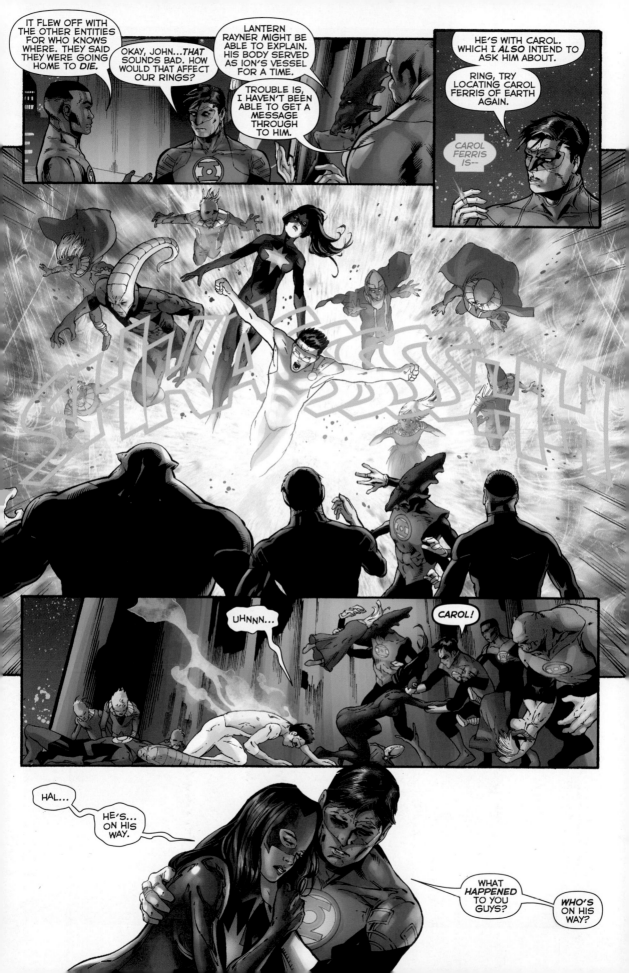

R-RELIC. HE CALLED HIMSELF *RELIC*.

"RELIC?" THAT DOESN'T SOUND SO BAD, KYLE.

HE SOUNDS *OLD*.

HE *IS* OLD. OLDER THAN EVERYTHING. HE'S SOME KIND OF SCIENTIST FROM THE UNIVERSE THAT EXISTED *BEFORE* OURS.

I SAW INSIDE HIS MIND, HAL. HE THINKS HIS UNIVERSE DIED BECAUSE ITS EMOTIONAL SPECTRUM *RAN OUT*.

SAY AGAIN?

HE THINKS THERE'S A *RESERVOIR* HOLDING A *FINITE* AMOUNT OF EMOTIONAL ENERGY, AND IT'S WHAT OUR RINGS AND BATTERIES TAP INTO.

WHEN THE RESERVOIR RUNS DRY... BANG. AS IN *BIG BANG*. THE UNIVERSE ENDS, AND A NEW ONE FORMS WITH A NEW RESERVOIR.

WHICH WOULD MEAN ANY TIME ANY LANTERN OF ANY CORPS HAS *EVER* USED A RING--

--WE'VE BEEN DESTROYING THE UNIVERSE.

PRETTY MUCH SUCKS TO THINK ABOUT, DOESN'T IT?

THE GREEN LANTERN CORPS HAS MAINTAINED ORDER THROUGHOUT THE UNIVERSE FOR MILLENNIA. WE'RE *PROTECTORS*, NOT DESTROYERS.

I WON'T BELIEVE OTHERWISE JUST BECAUSE SOME *LAB COAT* SAYS SO.

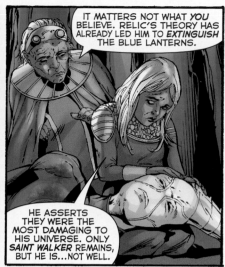

IT MATTERS NOT WHAT *YOU* BELIEVE. RELIC'S THEORY HAS ALREADY LED HIM TO *EXTINGUISH* THE BLUE LANTERNS.

HE ASSERTS THEY WERE THE MOST DAMAGING TO HIS UNIVERSE. ONLY *SAINT WALKER* REMAINS, BUT HE IS...NOT WELL.

THE BLUE LANTERNS ARE *GONE*?

I TRIED HEALING WALKER, BUT MY RING DOESN'T SEEM ABLE TO.

RELIC *INVADED* MY THOUGHTS, HAL. HE KNOWS WHAT I KNOW ABOUT THIS UNIVERSE'S USE OF THE EMOTIONAL SPECTRUM.

AND AS THE ONLY BEING TO EVER MASTER ALL SEVEN COLORS, I KNOW *A LOT*.

GUY...

WHAT *ABOUT* GUY?

HAL, THE GREEN LANTERNS ARE THE BIGGEST OF ALL THE CORPS. WE THINK RELIC HAS HIS SIGHTS SET ON OA NEXT. YOU NEED TO BE READY.

ONE GEEZER BEAT ALL OF YOU *AND* THE BLUE LANTERNS?

BY HIMSELF?

JUST ONE.

IN OUR DEFENSE--

NEW PLAN. KYLE AND CAROL, CONCENTRATE ON TAKING OUT RELIC'S COLLECTORS. START AT THE CENTRAL BATTERY AND WORK YOUR WAY OUT FROM THERE.

KILOWOG, LEAD THE REST OF THE LANTERNS. ESPECIALLY THE RECRUITS. WE DON'T NEED ANYONE PANICKING AT A TIME LIKE THIS.

I'LL KEEP 'EM IN LINE.

JOHN AND SALAAK, GET TO THE ARMORY AND SECURE THE LANTERN BATTERIES. WE'LL NEED THOSE CHARGES.

I'M A CHARISMATIC GUY.

WHAT ARE YOU GOING TO DO?

I KNOW HOW TO GET SOMEONE'S ATTENTION.

YOU KNOW, FOR A SECOND THERE, HE ACTUALLY SOUNDED LIKE THE CORPS LEADER.

LET'S GET TO WORK!

BROTHERS AND SISTERS, IF WHAT OCCURRED ON ELPIS OCCURS HERE...

WE MUST DELIVER WALKER TO SAFETY AND DEFEND THE CITADEL.

THEY ATE STRAIGHT THROUGH THE VAULT!

SAVE AS MANY BATTERIES AS YOU CAN!

NO...

...AM I *REALLY* SEEING WHAT I'M SEEING?

WE'RE DONE FOR.

THE CENTRAL POWER BATTERY IS *DEAD.*

SEE HOW QUICKLY YOUR *EWER* WAS EMPTIED? THIS UNIVERSE'S RESERVOIR MUST SURELY BE NEAR DEPLETION.

THE BATTERY IS EMPTY BECAUSE YOUR *ROBO-TICKS* BLED IT DRY.

YOU'VE GOT AN ACTIVE IMAGINATION, I'LL GIVE YOU THAT. BUT YOU'RE NO DIFFERENT FROM ANY OTHER *FREAK* WHO'S TRIED TO TAKE DOWN THE CORPS.

WE'VE BEATEN THEM ALL. WE'LL *BEAT* YOU.

VRZZZ

VRZZZ

VRZZZ

I'LL PUT YOUR LIGHT TO NOBLER USE THAN YOU EVER HAVE.

YOUR TIME OF *CONSUMPTION* IS FINISHED.

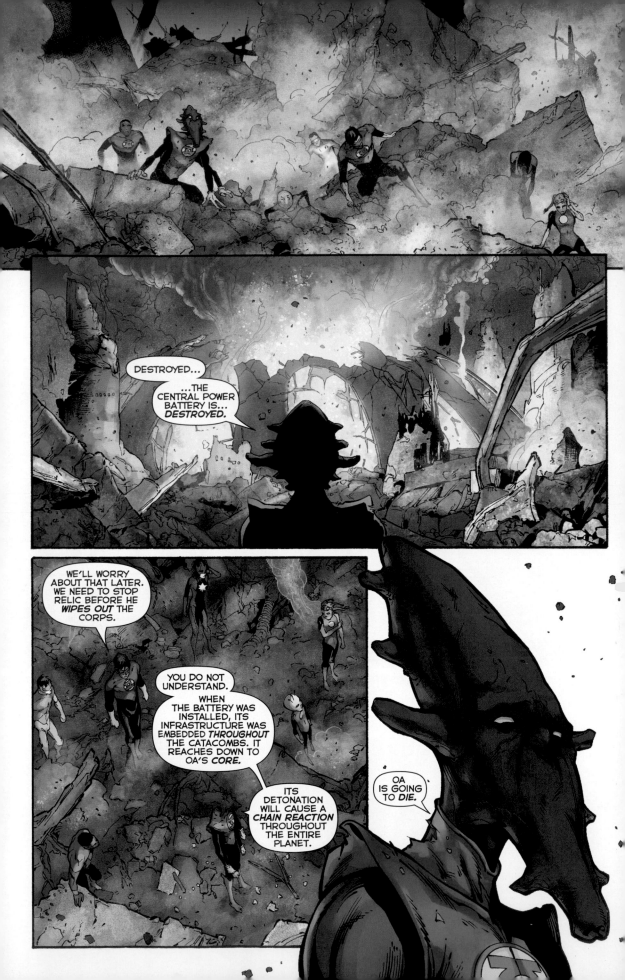

ELSEWHERE IN "LIGHTS OUT"...

Salaak's unbelievable prediction came true: the destruction of the Central Power Battery destabilized the very core of Oa. As the planet shook itself apart, Hal Jordan led a massive evacuation of the Green Lantern homeworld — and John Stewart and his untested new recruits covered their getaway by distracting Relic with an all-out assault. Ergann, the nomadic new Lantern of Sector 1234, gave his life to hold Relic back as Oa exploded... but Relic, unfortunately, survived. The rest of the Lanterns believed John's team to be lost as well — but instead of rejoining their comrades, John had taken his squad to Nok, the home of the mysterious Indigo Tribe.

Shaken by their loss, Hal Jordan decided to lead the Corps into the arms of the enemy: they would travel to Ysmault and seek help from the Red Lanterns, the dangerous maniacs that Hal had just sent Guy Gardner to infiltrate. But the universe had one more setback in store, as the fantastically powerful Entities, the living avatars of the emotional spectrum, suddenly arrived and possessed Kyle Rayner, sweeping the Green Lantern Corps away to Ysmault and taking Kyle away for their own purposes. It took the intervention of the New Guardians to break the Entities' control over Kyle, but with the Entities inside him, he now saw the conflict the way they did: Relic was right. The emotional spectrum was being depleted, and the universe would surely die as a result. Relic had taken up a post at the Source Wall, attempting to break through the barrier and into the reservoir beyond, with the intent of replenishing it... and Kyle and the Guardians would have to help him.

And on Ysmault, Hal Jordan and the Corps didn't receive the welcome they expected from Guy Gardner, who in his short time with the Red Lanterns had quickly gotten in over his head. His first spectacular outburst of rage had led to his beating their leader, Atrocitus, to the brink of death, and taking his red ring. Guy's influence on the Reds was uncertain, and he could only stay alive if they believed he was one of them and not still a Green Lantern in disguise — so an armada of Greens asking for help was the last thing he needed! To get the help of the Red Lanterns, Hal Jordan would have to offer them something in return — their own space sector to patrol, free of the influence of Green Lanterns. With that deal in place, the Red and Green Lanterns were tenuously united against Relic — but first, they had to find him...

ROBERT VENDITTI writer SEAN CHEN penciller JON SIBAL & WALDEN WONG inkers
cover art by SEAN CHEN, JON SIBAL & ALEX SINCLAIR

THE GREEN LANTERN I *BROKE SKULLS* WITH. MY *BEST FRIEND.*

YOU LET HIM DIE?

I DIDN'T *LET* HIM DO ANYTHING. HE VOLUNTEERED.

OUR RINGS ARE ON *FUMES*, AND WE DON'T HAVE ANY WAY TO RECHARGE.

JOHN TOOK A HANDFUL OF RECRUITS AND WENT *HEAD TO HEAD* WITH RELIC, SO THE REST OF US COULD ESCAPE.

WHERE IS THIS *RELIC?* I'LL TEAR OUT HIS THROAT AND *STRANGLE* HIM WITH IT!

THAT'S THE PROBLEM. WE THINK KYLE IS WITH HIM, BUT HIS RING IS BEING MASKED SOMEHOW. WE DON'T KNOW WHERE THEY ARE.

I MIGHT...

STAR SAPHIRE LOVE

...KNOW WHERE KYLE IS. MAYBE.

NO. ACTUALLY, I DO. I KNOW WHERE HE IS.

CAROL? HOW DO *YOU* KNOW WHERE KYLE IS?

DID HE TELL YOU WHERE HE WAS HEADED?

NOT EXACTLY. I JUST SORT OF... *FEEL* IT.

YOU... YOU'RE A STAR SAPPHIRE. YOUR RING IS POWERED BY *LOVE.*

AND YOU CAN FEEL WHERE *KYLE* IS?

AWKWARD.

NOW I SEE WHY YOU ENDED THINGS BETWEEN US. YOU GAVE A WHOLE SPEECH ABOUT ME NEEDING TO *GROW UP,* BUT WHAT YOU *REALLY* WANT IS KYLE!

SPEAKING OF *GROWING UP,* CAN YOU NOT DO THIS WHILE THE *FATE* OF *EVERY LANTERN* HANGS IN THE BALANCE?

...FAIR ENOUGH.

THANK YOU.

NOW GIVE ME SPACE, SO I CAN SEND OUT A TETHER.

ADVANCE WARNING, EVERYONE.

WHAT IF THE ENTITIES WERE WRONG TO LEAD ME HERE? WHAT IF THE RESERVOIR *ISN'T* ON THE OTHER SIDE OF THE WALL?

IT COULD BE ON A PLANET SOMEWHERE, OR INSIDE A QUASAR, OR--

NO!

I DEDICATED MY EXISTENCE TO FINDING MY UNIVERSE'S RESERVOIR. DISPATCHED PROBES TO COUNTLESS STARS AND WORLDS. TRAVELED TO EVERY CORNER.

ALL MY SEARCHES ENDED AT THE WALL.

RELEASE US!

THE RESERVOIR *IS* BEYOND THE WALL. IT MUST BE.

I WAS SURE I'D CAPTURED ENOUGH SPECTRUM ENERGY TO PIERCE IT, BUT PERHAPS YOU CAN GIVE ME WHAT I NEED.

STOP! WE WANT TO HELP YOU!

THE EMOTIONAL SPECTRUM IN LIVING FORM! OF COURSE!

COULD YOU *LIGHTBEASTS* HARBOR THE SPECTRUM ENERGY I SEEK?

DO NOT HARM THEM!

TO TAMPER WITH THE ENTITIES IS TO TAMPER WITH REALITY ITSELF!

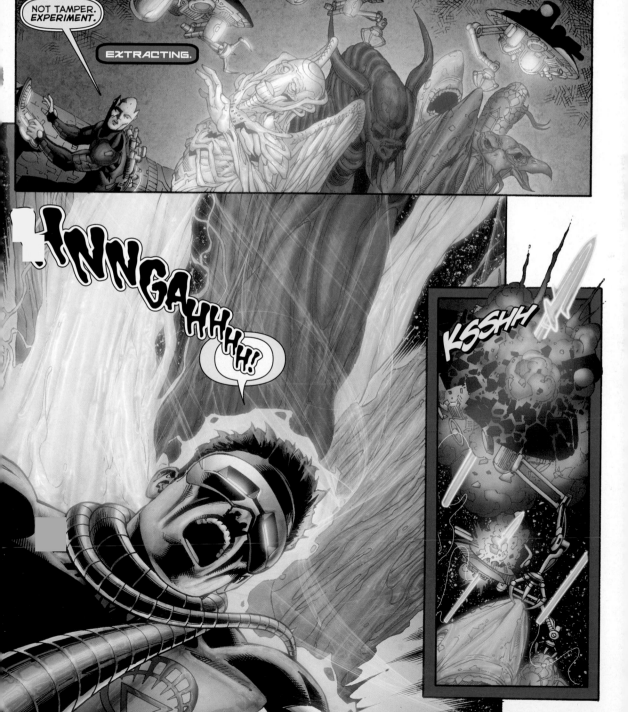

NOT TAMPER. EXPERIMENT.

EXTRACTING.

HNNGAHHHH!

KSSHH

THE WALL...IT TRAPS *EVERYTHING*.

RING, CHECK EVERYONE'S CHARGES. AND KEEP US UPDATED.

POWER LEVEL 5%.

POWER LEVEL 12%.

POWER LEVEL 6%.

POWER LEVEL 28%.

HEY, RAYNER. GET IN THE FIGHT, WHY DON'T YOU?

KYLE ASIDE, WE'VE GOT ENOUGH POWER FOR *ONE MORE* RUN. BUT WE CAN'T WASTE OUR CHARGES ON BLASTS OR CONSTRUCTS.

SO, YOU GUYS READY FOR A GAME OF GOOD OLD-FASHIONED *CHICKEN*?

INDIGO-1, CAN YOU TELEPORT US BETWEEN RELIC AND HIS REFLECTORS-- AND *KEEP* US THERE?

NOK.

GRAF? YOU'RE A LIGHT MONK. I KNOW *YOU* HAVEN'T FORGOTTEN THE OATH...

I CANNOT RECITE IT, HAL. NOT ANYMORE.

ME NEITHER.

NOR I.

WHY? WHAT'S THE MATTER WITH YOU?

DON'T YOU SEE? RELIC WAS RIGHT. WIELDING THE LIGHT *DOES* DEPLETE THE RESERVOIR OF THE EMOTIONAL SPECTRUM.

THE CLOCK IS ALREADY WINDING DOWN ON THE UNIVERSE'S SECOND LIFE. WE WON'T BE A PARTY TO SPEEDING IT UP.

KYLE MAY HAVE REPLENISHED THE RESERVOIR *THIS* TIME, BUT HE'S *GONE*...

LANTERN RAYNER'S DEATH IS A GREAT LOSS.

HE WAS A TRULY UNIQUE BEING. THERE IS SO MUCH MORE HE MIGHT HAVE TAUGHT US. AND WE, HIM.

HOW WAS HE ABLE TO PASS BEYOND THE WALL, PAALKO? HAVE YOU EVER HEARD OF SUCH A THING?

NOT IN ALL MY EONS. MORE INTRIGUING STILL...WHAT WAITS TO BE DISCOVERED ON THE OTHER SIDE?

WE DEPARTED OA TO LEARN ABOUT THE UNIVERSE. IS THERE A GREATER QUESTION THAN THIS?

?

FWASH

MUST YOU POKE *EVERYTHING* WITH A STICK?

I DID NOT TOUCH IT, ZALLA! I ONLY *ALMOST* DID!

FWASHHH

COULD IT BE...?

NYAAGH!

UHNNHN.

LANTERN RAYNER!

WHAT OCCURRED? *TELL US!*

THE ENTITIES... THEY *SACRIFICED* THEMSELVES. THEY SAID IT WAS THE ONLY WAY TO REFILL THE RESERVOIR.

THEY'RE... DEAD.

WHAT *ELSE*, LANTERN RAYNER? *ALL* YOU WITNESSED. *ALL* YOU EXPERIENCED. WE MUST KNOW *EVERYTHING!*

ROBERT VENDITTI writer BILLY TAN penciller ROB HUNTER inker
cover art by BILLY TAN & ALEX SINCLAIR

DON'T YOU THINK YOU'RE OVERREACTING? WE CAN'T BE SURE *WHAT* HAPPENED AT THE SOURCE WALL.

AND EVEN IF THERE *IS* A RESERVOIR OF LIGHT, IT TOOK *BILLIONS* OF YEARS FOR IT TO RUN DRY. THE GAS TANK IS *FULL* NOW.

THERE'LL BE PLENTY OF TOMORROWS TO WORRY ABOUT ITS EMPTYING AGAIN. WE SHOULD FOCUS ON THE THREATS FACING US *TODAY*.

FOR MOST OF THOSE YEARS, THE GREEN LANTERNS WERE THE ONLY CORPS. NOW THERE ARE *MANY*.

HE'S RIGHT, HAL. THE COUNTDOWN TIMER HAS SPED UP.

THAT'S WHY WE'RE NEEDED MORE THAN EVER, TOMAR-TU. THE BLUE LANTERNS ARE *GONE*. THE BALANCE OF THE SPECTRUM HAS BEEN TIPPED.

COMPASSIONATE AS THE INDIGO TRIBE IS, THEY'RE ONLY ONE RING CHARGE AWAY FROM REVERTING TO THEIR MURDEROUS, *PSYCHO-PATHIC* SELVES.

AND THE STAR SAPPHIRES ONLY LOVE US *SOMETIMES*.

SUBTLE, HAL.

GOOD GUYS ARE *SCARCE*. WE SHELVE OUR RINGS, WHAT HAPPENS TO THE REST OF THE UNIVERSE?

YOU THINK THE *SINESTRO* CORPS IS GOING TO STAY *AWOL* FOREVER? OR THAT *LARFLEEZE* WILL QUIT HOARDING LIGHT FOR HIMSELF?

GREEN LANTERNS ARE CHOSEN FOR THEIR WILLPOWER, YET YOU ATTEMPT TO SWAY US WHEN WE'VE ALREADY MADE UP OUR MINDS.

I CANNOT HELP BUT NOTICE THE CONTRADICTION.

ALL RIGHT, GRAF. IF YOUR CHOICE IS BASED ON CONVICTION, I WON'T HOLD IT AGAINST YOU.

THAT GOES FOR ANY OF YOU. BUT REMEMBER, WE'VE ALL SWORN AN OATH TO PROTECT THE UNIVERSE, AND THAT'S *EXACTLY* WHAT WE'RE GOING TO DO.

AS CORPS LEADER, I'M ISSUING A NEW *PRIMARY OBJECTIVE*: IT'S TIME WE STARTED *POLICING* THE USE OF THE EMOTIONAL SPECTRUM.

WHAT?

WHEN EVERY LANTERN OF EVERY COLOR HAS STOPPED USING LIGHT, WE CAN *ALL* PUT DOWN OUR RINGS. UNTIL THEN, UNAUTHORIZED RING WEARERS GET ARRESTED AND TRIED FOR VIOLATION OF THE UNIVERSAL CRIMINAL CODE.

STARTING *NOW*.

-AHEM-

GUESS WHICH *FINGER* I'M HOLDING UP.

CAROL. RIGHT. I, UM...

YOU *WHAT,* HAL? YOU'RE GOING TO ELABORATE ON WHAT EXACTLY CONSTITUTES AN *UNAUTHORIZED* RING WEARER?

WHY DO I GET THE FEELING IT'S ANYONE WHO ISN'T DECKED OUT IN *GREEN?*

LOOK, IF KYLE SACRIFICING HIMSELF REALLY *DID* REFILL THE RESERVOIR, THEN HE GAVE US A SECOND CHANCE. A CHANCE TO DO THINGS *BETTER* THIS TIME.

EXACTLY. HE GAVE *US* A SECOND CHANCE. *ALL* OF US.

AND SINCE THERE ISN'T ANOTHER WHITE LANTERN LIKE HIM, THIS MAY BE OUR *LAST* CHANCE.

CAN WE TALK ABOUT THIS SOMEWHERE MORE *PRIVATE?*

I'M SORRY. AM I MAKING YOU LOOK BAD IN FRONT OF THE FELLAS?

MAYBE YOU'D PREFER THAT I HAND OVER MY RING IN SERVICE OF YOUR *HALF-BAKED* PLAN DU JOUR.

OR WOULD YOU RATHER I JOIN UP WITH YOU? HELP YOU SCOUR THE UNIVERSE UNTIL ALL THE GREEN LANTERN CORPS' ENEMIES ARE LOCKED AWAY?

"—AND NOT EVEN *CAROL* WILL MIND US STRIPPING THE RING FROM THIS ONE."

OUTER RIM OF SPACE SECTOR 0563. THE PLANET DEKANN.

THIS IS HOW IT OUGHTA BE.

BUSINESS CRATERED THESE PAST MONTHS, BRAIDMEN, BUT WE'RE *BRIM-FULL* NOW.

SKIN TRADE, CONTRABAND, OFF-ORANX BETTING...ALL *UP.* THE PRIXIAM WILL BE MOST SATISFIED.

WHAT DO YOU S'POSE MADE THE SWITCH, GRANACK?

WHY CARE? PEOPLE TROLLING THE CIRC TO INDULGE IN OUR SERVICES...*THAT* I'M INTERESTED IN. NOT INDULGING IS AS ALIEN TO ME AS PROPER ETIQUETTE.

COUNT THIS UP AND CRATE IT. IT'S ALREADY NEEDED FOR PASS-AROUND.

MAKE SURE THE TALLY IS ACCURATE.

YOU WHO THREATENS MY CLANN! **SHOW YOURSELF!**

YOU'RE AN EASY MARK, GRANACK. GUESS IT DOESN'T TAKE MUCH TO CONVINCE THOSE WHO PREY ON *WEAKNESS* THAT OTHERS WILL DO THE SAME.

DON'T--!

KRNCH

I GOT WHAT I NEEDED, AND ALL IT COST YOU WAS A *HAIRCUT.*

AND SOME PEBBLE-SHOOTERS.

TOOK YOU LONGER THAN I EXPECTED, NOL-ANJ. MAYBE YOU DON'T LOVE YOUR FOOT SOLDIERS AS MUCH AS YOU PRETEND.

OR DID I *OVERESTIMATE* YOUR SKILL WITH THE VIOLET LIGHT?

MY SKILL BROUGHT YOU TO YOUR *KNEES* ONCE BEFORE, GREEN LANTERN.

--IT'S ANOTHER COUNT ADDED TO THE INDICTMENT.

I ACT IN SERVICE TO MY *CLANN*. ALWAYS. AS A PRIXIAM IS DUTY BOUND TO DO.

WHAT YOU LABEL AS CRIMES, MY PEOPLE SEE AS ACTS OF *LOVE*.

A LOVE THAT WAS VALIDATED WHEN A STAR SAPPHIRE'S RING CHOSE *ME* AS ITS WEARER.

SPEAKING OF BOLOVAX VIK, WHAT WE GOT HERE IS A CRAB INDIGENOUS TO THE SLOODLE MARSH. I'VE ENLARGED IT FOR YOUR PERUSAL.

NOTICE THE BIGGER FORE-CLAWS, USED FOR HOLDING PREY WHILE THE SECOND AND THIRD SETS TEAR OFF BITE-SIZED CHUNKS FOR EATING.

BEAUTIFUL, AIN'T SHE?

ROBERT VENDITTI writer BILLY TAN penciller ROB HUNTER, DON HO & BILLY TAN inkers
cover art by BILLY TAN & ALEX SINCLAIR

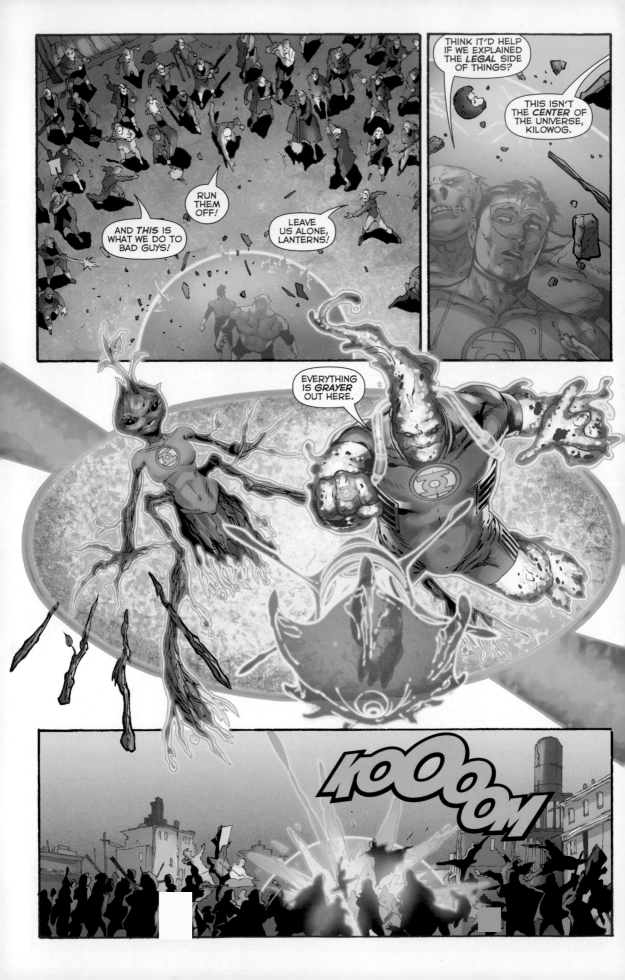

I WANTED TO MAKE AN *EXAMPLE* OF NOL-ANJ. LET OTHERS KNOW THE ERA OF WASTING LIGHT IS *OVER.*

INSTEAD, THE ONLY EXAMPLE WE SET WAS OURS. AND IT'S A *BAD* ONE.

WE'LL GET THERE, JORDAN. THERE'S ALWAYS MORE JEWELRY TO CHASE DOWN.

AND DON'T FRET THE MESSAGING. NO ONE'LL HEAR ABOUT THIS.

"NEWS NEVER LEAVES THE CIRC."

THE LANTERNS ARE ARRESTING *ALL* OF DEKANN'S BRAIDMEN...

SLURRRRKK

YES.

THE OUTCOME IS BETTER THAN WE'D HOPED.

SLURRRRKK

I RECEIVED WORD, BROTHER. THE FOUR-ARMED ONE IS EN ROUTE WITH THEIR FORTRESS.

NOTIFY THE ANCIENTS.

TELL THEM TO READY THE NEXT PHASE.